The Afterlife Confirmed

Even More Convincing Evidence
From The Survival Files

The Afterlife Confirmed

Even More Convincing Evidence
From The Survival Files

by
Miles Edward Allen

Momentpoint Media

The Afterlife Confirmed

Cover: A statue of Maj. General George G. Meade
overlooks Gettysburg battlefields.
Photo and cover design by Miles Edward Allen.

Ignorance is king. Many would not profit by his abdication. Many enrich themselves by means of his dark monarchy. They are his Court, and in his name they defraud and govern, enrich themselves and perpetuate their power.

— Walter M. Miller, Jr.
A Canticle for Leibowitz

Contents

This book is dedicated
to all those who have given freely
of their time and resources
to support the work of
AECES
(The Association for Evaluation and Communication
of Evidence for Survival)
www.aeces.info

As with the prequel to this book,
the "old man" is fanciful,
the conversations are speculative,
but the cases are, to the best of my knowledge,
factual and accurate accounts of real events.

Chapter One

A Gettysburg Gathering

The public was being protected against all knowledge of the inexplicable, the weird, the surrealistic. All part of the usual governmental pretense that human affairs were rationally administered by experts who knew what was really going on. They feared that if people ever discovered that those in power were as confused by this inexplicable universe as those out of power, then the whole charade might collapse.

— Robert Anton Wilson
Schrodinger's Cat

The rain had stopped in the morning, but the sunshine on the green fields and split-log fences did little to brighten our somber mood. For the moment, there were no busses on the gravel pullover and no crowds of school children or camera-toting tourists milling about beside us; we stood quietly alone, reluctant to challenge the majestic silence of the lands that stretched before us. They were anything but silent during the first three days of July in 1863 as more than 51,000 soldiers died or were wounded here.

Two years and more had passed since I spent a weekend being tutored by "the old man" not so far from here, at his cabin in the Appalachian hills. We had kept somewhat in touch, meeting occasionally at charitable functions in D.C. Today, we were visiting the battlefields as a prelude to a conference on the afterlife being held in historic Gettysburg, Pennsylvania. It seemed to me only fitting to speak about the Survival of death at a place known for the deaths of so many in such a brief time. Finally, the old man broke the somber mood.

> "Remind you of anything?" he asked, looking down at two dead mice semi-submerged in a small pool of rainwater at the bottom of a grassy slope.

They were lying in a line, nose to tail, as if they had been playing follow-the-leader and the first one had died so the second followed suit. They had wandered pretty far from the McPherson barn to have dined on poison there, but I could think of no other reason for their demise. I was tempted to say something about them being overcome with grief at the horrendous loss of life on this field where the battle of Gettysburg had started, but the place didn't seem right for any form of levity. So, I just gave him a questioning glance.

> "At the cabin, we considered several OBEs. We decided to call them 'Other-Body Experiences'."

"I recall being especially impressed with the OBEs of the children and folks who are blind."

"Just so. And do you recall also why we thought that OBEs in the blind might provide special evidence for Survival?"

"I do. We speculated that the experiential referents necessary for the blind to recognize physical images must have been learned prior to their birth."

"Your memory is excellent," he said.

"Well, maybe, but I don't recall any link between OBEs and dead rodents."

He reached over and patted my forearm in such an avuncular manner that I half expected him to say "Tut, tut, my good man." But he just smiled a bit and, after looking a while longer at the grassy hills, asked "What do you think of the OBEs of sighted adults as evidence for a life beyond?"

I considered this as we turned and walked back towards our rental car. Best I could recall, when at his cabin, we hadn't talked much about the evidential value of OBEs. When I wrote up our conversation, I included a quote from Robert Crookall to the effect that being able to temporarily leave one's body was a good indication that one could perform the same feat after the body died. Beyond that, I hadn't thought much about the matter, and I told him so.

"Let's say that you live in Orlando and have the sensation of leaving your physical body and traveling to Osaka. It is true that being able to accomplish this feat while your body is alive does not guarantee that you will be able to repeat the performance after the body's demise. No, it does not guarantee it, but it does suggest it very strongly. If the very existence of your mind was dependent upon your physical body being alive, then there would have to be some physical mechanism of dependence operating between your body in Florida and your mind in Japan. But such a connection doesn't exist. There are neither blood-filled arteries nor strands of nerves stretching across the Pacific. No electrical signals or light rays flicker between your mind and the body it left behind."

"But there does seem to be some sort of connection," I pointed out. "Many astral travelers have reported that a disturbance or discomfort of their body causes their mind to snap back from wherever it has journeyed."

"Which indicates that the OBEr's mind remains somewhat aware of their body; but awareness isn't the same as dependence.

"Any observation mechanism must have a viewpoint and perspective and scale. But this mechanism cannot be physical or we could detect it with physical instruments."

"I well remember the astral eyes," I said.[1]

> "Indeed. And if something isn't physical, how can it be dependent upon a physical process? I really don't see any good reason to suspect that the cessation of physical processes in the body (which we call death) should have any effect upon these non-physical (astral) mechanisms."

"So the ability of some people to travel out-of-body is, truly, additional evidence for the ability of us all to survive the grave."

> "Seems a fair and reasonable conclusion to me.
>
> "And that grave we will survive brings us back to the mice."

We had reached the car, so I took advantage of the time to get it started and fasten my seatbelt to consider that reference, then: "Ah, yes! Now I remember. I shall have to include that story in my next book."

Here is the case we were referring to. I present it exactly as it was written by Robert Dale Owen, just after the Civil War ended.[2]

---

[1] See *The Survival Files*, p. 58.

[2] Owen, Robert, *Footfalls on the Boundary of Another World*, 1868, pp. 178-180.

The Two Field-Mice

"In the winter of 1835-36, a schooner was frozen up in the upper part of the Bay of Fundy, close to Dorchester, which is nine miles from the river Pedeudiac. During the time of her detention she was intrusted to the care of a gentleman of the name of Clarke, who is at this time captain of the schooner Julia Hallock, trading between New York and St. Jago de Cuba.

"Captain Clarke's paternal grandmother, Mrs. Ann Dawe Clarke, to whom he was much attached, was at that time living, and, so far as he knew, well. She was residing at Lyme-Regis, in the county of Dorset, England.

"On the night of the 17th of February, 1836, Captain Clarke, then on board the schooner referred to, had a dream of so vivid a character that it produced a great impression upon him. He dreamed that, being at Lyme- Regis, he saw pass before him the funeral of his grandmother. He took note of the chief persons who composed the procession, observed who were the pall-bearers, who were the mourners, and in what order they walked, and distinguished who was the officiating pastor. He joined the procession as it approached the churchyard gate, and proceeded with it to the grave. He thought (in his dream) that the weather was stormy, and the ground wet, as after a heavy rain; and he noticed that the wind, being high, blew the pall partly off the coffin. The graveyard which they entered, the old Protestant one, in the center of the town, was the same in which, as Captain Clarke knew, their family burying-place was. He perfectly remembered its situation; but, to his surprise, the funeral procession did not proceed thither, but to another part of the churchyard, at some distance. There (still in his dream) he saw the open grave, partially filled with water, as from the rain; and, looking into it, he particularly noticed floating in the water two drowned field-mice. Afterward, as he thought, he conversed with his mother; and she told him that the morning had been so tempestuous that the funeral, originally appointed for ten o'clock, had been deferred till four. He remarked, in reply, that it was a fortunate circumstance; for, as he had just arrived in time to join the procession, had the funeral taken place in the forenoon he could not have attended it at all.

"This dream made so deep an impression on Captain Clarke that in the morning he noted the date of it. Some time afterward there came the news of his grandmother's death, with the additional particular that she was buried on the same day on which he, being in North America, had dreamed of her funeral.

"When, four years afterward, Captain Clarke visited Lyme-Regis, he found that every particular of his dream minutely corresponded with the reality. The pastor, the pall-bearers, the mourners, were the same persons he had seen. Yet this, we may suppose, he might naturally have anticipated. But the funeral had been appointed for ten o'clock in the morning, and, in consequence of the tempestuous weather and the heavy rain that was falling, it had been delayed until four in the afternoon. His mother, who attended the funeral, distinctly recollected that the high wind blew the pall partially off the coffin. In consequence of a wish expressed by the old lady shortly before her death, she was buried, not in the burying-place of the family, but at another spot, selected by herself; and to this spot Captain Clarke, without any indication from the family or otherwise, proceeded at once, as directly as if he had been present at the burial. Finally, on comparing notes with the old sexton, it appeared that the heavy rain of the morning had partially filled the grave, and that there were actually found in it two field-mice, drowned.

"This last incident, even if there were no other, might suffice to preclude all idea of accidental coincidence.

"The above was narrated to me by Captain Clarke himself;* [Footnote in Owen's text: * In New York, on July 28, 1859. The narrative is written out from notes taken on board his schooner.] with permission to use his name in attestation of its truth."

On the way back to Lincoln Square, we agreed that Captain Clarke's tale is not strong evidence of Survival, as it could simply be the result of an other-body experience. But OBEs such as his certainly support the idea of an independent spirit and thus of its ability to endure beyond the demise of the physical body. When the vast amount of such supporting evidence is considered, those cases that do provide solid evidence for Survival become even more convincing. Throughout this book, I will present some of the most convincing evidence for an afterlife as listed in the current Survival Top 40. (See www.survivaltop40.com or www.aeces .info for more about this list and Survival evidence in general.) Interspersed among these top cases, I shall relate our discussions of some implications and intriguing aspects of evidence of the supporting type.

A note on the organization of the following material: Throughout our three-day stay in Gettysburg, the old man and I had several opportunities to discuss matters both weighty and mundane. Unlike the course of instruction that I was privileged to receive at his cabin, these talks were unscheduled and unstructured, so presenting them as they happened would likely be more confusing than enlightening. Prepare yourself, therefore, for anything.

We parked in the garage behind the hotel and walked up the shady side of the street towards the main entrance.

"Being in this historic city," he said, as his walking stick tapped along the concrete walk, "it occurs to me, that you might set the scene for this new book of yours with a bit of history."

"The history of psychic phenomena is a huge subject," I replied, as we rounded the corner into the sunlight and started up the wide brick stairs. "Did you have any particular approach in mind?"

"Well, I suppose you could start with the prophets of old, but you'd likely lose half your readers before you got to Delphi. Perhaps a few words about rapping would be both enlightening and entertaining," he said, punctuating the word "rapping" by tapping the head of his stick on the frame of the large glass doors to the lobby of the Gettysburg Hotel.

Chapter Two

Knock, Knock …

When faced with evidence against their will,
They keep the same opinion still.

— Anonymous

Unexplained physical activities – knockings, flying objects, and such – have been reported throughout history. So numerous and common are they, that several languages have coined words specifically to denote them, including the German "poltergeister" — meaning "rumbling (or noisy) spirit" — from which, of course, English speakers have derived "poltergeist."

There are three popular explanations for poltergeist activity. Fans of contemporary horror movies might agree with Catholic priests of previous centuries that poltergeists are manifestations of Satan or, at least, of one of his demonic hoard. As organized efforts in occult research were getting underway in the 19th century, investigators noted the rather playful aspect of many outbreaks and tended to think in terms of "tricksy elves" or "imps of frolic and misrule." As the new science of psychology came of age in the 20th century, the focus shifted to a supposed correlation between the disturbances and the presence of pubescent youths. The idea here being that repressed sexual energy was being released in bursts of kinetic activity. This approach remains popular in contemporary thought; though an examination of the facts reveals that frustrated libidos alone are insufficient to explain the phenomena.

Let's look at a few representative, and fascinating, cases occurring over the past 450 years.

Terror at Tedworth[3]

Mr. John Mompesson was a justice of the peace of excellent reputation with deep familial roots in the south of England. One day in mid-April, 1661, when Mompesson returned to his home in Tedworth from a trip to London, he found his household in an uproar. His wife claimed that, during the previous night, loud and frightening noises had been heard as if vandals were destroying the place. Mompesson was concerned but puzzled, as there were no signs of forced entry and nothing seemed to be damaged or missing.

---

[3] This case is based on a narrative written by the Reverend Joseph Glanvil, chaplain to King Charles II and a Fellow of the Royal Society, based on his personal observations and on testimony provided directly to him by the principal of the case. "Tedworth," now Tidworth, lies just north of Salisbury, England.

A few nights later, he experienced the phenomena for himself, when his rest was shattered by very loud knocks on the doors and walls of his house. Jumping from bed in alarm, he grabbed his pistols and went to investigate. He opened each door and went around the outside of his house but could detect no cause for the banging. When he returned to his bed, more puzzled than ever, the thumping seemed to come from the roof. Finally, it faded away, seemingly into the night sky.

This was the beginning of a two-year siege during which the family was terrorized by hundreds of intrusions of an astonishing assortment including:

- Knocks both outside and inside the house, knocks loud enough to make the floor shake and the windows rattle, many so loud that they awakened the neighbors in the not-so-nearby village. The sounds generally started within a half-hour of the household's retirement for the night and continued for two or more hours.
- Drum beats, often of well-known patterns. One witnesses claimed that the phantom drummer would honor requests and play particular beats.
- Scratching beneath and behind beds.
- Ferocious banging on the children's beds of such violence that all present expected the beds to fall apart.
- Chairs and stools moving about when no one was near them.

• Shoes, bedstaves,[4] and other small items being hurled around the room with no apparent motive force.

These and other mysterious events were witnessed by numerous people of every social rank, nearly always on calm, clear nights. Despite almost constant vigilance and thorough investigations, no natural cause could be detected. But it didn't take long for Mr. Mompesson to decide what, or rather who, was likely the unnatural cause.

It seems that just a month before his troubles began, Mompesson was in the town of Ludgershall, a couple of miles from his home, when he had cause to examine the papers of a vagrant who had been annoying the local citizenry by loudly banging a drum and demanding alms. The vagrant's name was William Drury and the beggars permit he proffered had clearly been forged, so Mompesson had the drum confiscated. Leaving Drury in the custody of the local constable, and the drum in the custody of the bailiff, Mompesson returned to his home and shortly forgot about the supposedly inconsequential incident. The drummer was soon released, but the bailiff, being uncertain what to do with the drum, decided to send it to Mompesson. It

---

[4] A bedstaff is a wooden pin used to hold bedclothes to the frame.

had arrived at the JP's house in mid-April, just as he was leaving on his trip to London.

It didn't take long for Mompesson to become convinced that Drury was the cause of all his troubles, so he had the drummer arrested on a charge of witchcraft. Drury was not convicted of being a witch, but he was put on trial, and his trial provided opportunity for numerous witnesses to testify under oath as to the events they had observed.

Überskeptics have typically tried to laugh off this case as being too incredible to bother disputing. If it stood alone, they would have my support. But there are many such cases.

Another popular evasion is to quote from a book by Charles MacKay[5] who, in 1858, concluded that Mompesson's trouble was obviously caused by gypsy cohorts of the drummer. Being concerned with the nutty things people will do when part of a group, MacKay focused on how the events at Tedworth may have been inflated by excited servants, peasants, and children — as such stories typically are. In trying to chalk it all up to gullibility and fraud, however, MacKay conveniently forgets to tell his readers just how a band of gypsies managed to move all manner of household items

---

[5] Mackay, Charles, *Extraordinary Popular Delusions and the Madness of Crowds*, first published 1841, reprint Harriman House, 2003.

through the air of a child's bedroom without being seen by several intent observers. Neither did he suggest how they accomplished, in a similar invisible mode, the feat of striking a bed so hard that the floors shook and the windows rattled. Überskeptics, of course, are typically good at claiming something was a trick, but a bit weak on explaining how the trick might have been executed.

It is also noteworthy that no critic has ever suggested where this band of pranksters might have been living throughout the two years that the disturbances continued. It was, after all, a very close-knit community, and any strangers in the neighborhood would surely have been noticed. In fact, there was never any indication that Drury had any co-conspirators, nor has any motive been suggested beyond the rather petty one of the confiscated drum.

Those who'd like to think that Mompesson himself contrived the entire pageant should first consider these words of chaplain Glanvil's:

"[Mr. Mompesson] suffered by it in his name, in his estate, in all his affairs, and in the general peace of his family The unbelievers in the matter of spirits and witches took him for an impostor. Many others judged the permission of such an extraordinary evil to be the judgment of God upon him for some notorious wickedness or impiety. Thus his name was continually exposed to censure, and his estate suffered by the concourse of people from all parts to his house; by the diversion it gave him from his affairs; by the discouragement of servants, by reason of which he could hardly get any to live with him. To which I add, the continual hurry that his family was in, the affrights, and the watchings and disturbance of his whole house (in which himself must needs be the most concerned). I say, if these things are considered, there will be little reason to think he would have any interest to put a cheat upon the world in which he would most of all have injured and abused himself."[6]

An Excitement at Epworth[7]

Advancing a half century or so, we have a report written by a 17-year-old Englishman, the fifteenth of nineteen children born to a highly educated and immensely respected family. Because this young man was away at boarding school during most of the occurrences, his report is based on interviews of, and written testimonies he collected from, his own family members and neighbors. I have attempted to shorten the account

---

[6] Glanvil, Joseph, *Sadducismus Triumphatus*, London, 1689, p. 334.

[7] This presentation is based on numerous documents, foremost among which are Robert Dale Owen's *Footfalls on the Boundary of Another World*, and Dudley Wright's *The Epworth Phenomena*.

a bit by deleting minor and repetitive statements, but the majority is well worth quoting — and studying.

The young man writes: "On December 2, 1716, while Robert Brown, my father's servant, was sitting with one of the maids, a little before ten at night, in the dining-room, which opened into the garden, they both heard one knocking at the door. Robert rose and opened it, but could see nobody. Quickly it knocked again, and groaned. 'It is Mr. Turpine,' said Robert: 'he has the stone, and uses to groan so.' He opened the door again twice or thrice, the knocking being twice or thrice repeated; but, still seeing nothing, and being a little startled, they rose up and went to bed.

"When Robert came to the top of the garret stairs, he saw a handmill which was at a little distance whirled about very swiftly. When he related this he said, 'Nought vexed me but that it was empty. I thought if it had but been full of malt he might have ground his heart out for me.' When he was in bed, he heard as it were the gobbling of a turkey-cock close to the bedside, and soon after the sound of one stumbling over his shoes and boots; but there was none there: he had left them below.

"The next day, he and the maid related these things to the other maid, who laughed heartily, and said, 'What a couple of fools are you! I defy any thing to fright me.' After churning in the evening, she put the butter in the tray, and had no sooner carried it into the dairy than she heard a knocking on the shelf where several puncheons[8] of milk stood, first above the shelf, then below. She took the candle, and searched both above and below, but, being able to find nothing, threw down butter, tray and all, and ran away for life.

"The next evening, between five and six o'clock, my sister Molly, then about twenty years of age, sitting in the dining-room reading, heard as if it were the door that led into the hall open, and a person walking in that seemed to have on a silk night-gown, rustling and trailing along. It seemed to walk round her, then to the door, then round again; but she could see nothing. She thought, 'It signifies nothing to run away; for, whatever it is, it can run faster than me.' So she rose, put her book under her arm, and walked slowly away.

"After supper, she was sitting with my sister Sukey (about a year older than her) in one of the chambers, and telling her what had happened. She made quite light of it, telling her, 'I wonder you are so easily frighted: I would fain see what would fright me.' Presently a knocking began under the table. She took the candle and looked, but could find nothing. Then the iron casement began to clatter, and the lid of a warming-pan. Next the latch of the door moved up and down without ceasing. She started up, leaped into

---

[8] A puncheon is a cask that holds about 84 gallons (318 liters).

the bed without undressing, pulled the bed-clothes over her head, and never ventured to look up until next morning.

"A night or two after, my sister Hetty (a year younger than my sister Molly) was waiting as usual, between nine and ten, to take away my father's candle, when she heard one coming down the garret stairs, walking slowly by her, then going down the best stairs, then up the back stairs, and up the garret stairs and at every step it seemed the house shook from top to bottom. Just then my father knocked. She went in, took his candle, and got to bed as fast as possible. In the morning she told this to my eldest sister, who told her, 'You know I believe none of these things: pray let me take away the candle to-night, and I will find out the trick.' She accordingly took my sister Hetty's place, and had no sooner taken away the candle than she heard a noise below. She hastened down stairs to the hall, where the noise was, but it was then in the kitchen. She ran into the kitchen, where it was drumming on the inside of the screen. When she went round, it was drumming on the outside, and so always on the side opposite to her. Then she heard a knocking at the back kitchen door. She ran to it, unlocked it softly, and, when the knocking was repeated, suddenly opened it; but nothing was to be seen. As soon as she had shut it, the knocking began again. She opened it again but could see nothing. When she went to shut the door, it was violently thrust against her; but she set her knee and her shoulder to the door, forced it to, and turned the key. Then the knocking began again; but she let it go on, and went up to bed. However, from that time she was thoroughly convinced that there was no imposture in the affair.

"The next morning, my sister telling my mother what had happened, she said, 'If I hear any thing myself, I shall know how to judge.' Soon after she begged her to come into the nursery. She did, and heard, in the corner of the room, as it were the violent rocking of a cradle; but no cradle had been there for some years. She was convinced it was preternatural, and earnestly prayed it might not disturb her in her own chamber at the hours of retirement; and it never did. She now thought it was proper to tell my father. But he was extremely angry, and said, 'Sukey, I am ashamed of you. These boys and girls frighten one another; but you are a woman of sense, and should know better. Let me hear of it no more.'

"At six in the evening he had family prayers as usual. When he began the prayer for the king, a knocking began all round the room, and a thundering knock attended the Amen. The same was heard from this time every morning and evening while the prayer for the king was repeated.

"Mr. Hoole, the vicar of Haxey (an eminently pious and sensible man) — said, 'Robert Brown came over to me, and told me your father desired my company. When I came, he gave me an account of all that had happened, particularly the knocking during family prayer. But that evening (to my great satisfaction) we had no knocking at all. But between nine and ten a servant came in, and said, "Old Jeffrey is coming," (that was the name of one that died in the house) "for I hear the signal." This, they informed me, was heard every night about a quarter before ten. It was toward the top of the house, on the outside, at the northeast corner, resembling the loud creaking of a saw, or rather that of a windmill when the body of it is turned about in order to shift the sails to the wind. We then heard a knocking over our heads; and [your father], catching up a candle, said, "Come, sir, now you shall hear for yourself." We went upstairs; he with much hope, and I (to say the truth) with much fear. When we came into the nursery, it was knocking in the next room; when we went there, it was knocking in the nursery. And there it continued to knock, though we came in, particularly at the head of the bed (which was of wood). He then said, sternly, "Thou deaf and dumb devil! Why dost thou fright these children, that cannot answer for themselves? Come to me, in my study, that am a man!" Instantly, it knocked his knock (the particular knock which he always used) and we heard nothing more that night.'

"Till this time my father had never heard the least disturbance in his study. But the next evening, as he attempted to go into his study (of which none had the key but himself) when he opened the door, it was thrust back with such violence as had like to have thrown him down. However, he thrust the door open, and went in. Presently there was a knocking, first on one side, then on the other, and, after a time, in the next room, wherein my sister Nancy was. He went into that room, and, the noise continuing, adjured it to speak, but in vain."

There is more to this account, but the incidents described therein are of essentially the same character as those related above. And who was this young gentleman who tells such haunting tales? He was John Wesley, later to be known as the patriarch of the Methodist church. His father was the Reverend Samuel Wesley, the rector of Epworth, England, and the disturbances took place at the parsonage there. The testimony above has been extensively corroborated, mainly by a journal that Samuel Wesley kept at the time and by numerous letters written by eyewitnesses. A few incidents described in those documents may be of interest here.

Samuel Wesley's journal entries include two occasions when the knockings seemed to respond in kind to knocks made by he and his children. On three occasions, he notes, he was "pushed by an invisible power, once against the corner of my desk in the study, a second time against the door of the matted chamber, a third time against the right side of the frame of my study door, as I was going in." His entry on Christmas Day states that their household dog, a mastiff, "came whining to us," as he did at every occurrence except for the initial incident when the dog "barked violently." That mastiff, Samuel wrote, "seemed more afraid than any of the children."

Mrs. Susanna Wesley, in a letter to John, wrote that once she had the idea that if the intruder was a spirit it might answer her, and so she stamped several times on the floor. In return, she says, "it repeated under the sole of my feet exactly the same number of strokes, with the very same intervals."

Emily Wesley later wrote in a letter that the presence "would knock when I was putting the children to bed, just under me, where I sat. One time little Kezzy, pretending to scare Polly, as I was undressing them, stamped with her foot on the floor; and immediately it answered with three knocks, just in the same place. It was more loud and fierce if any one said it was rats, or any thing natural."

It is difficult for the fair-minded person to disagree with one of Wesley's biographers who concluded: "The accounts given of these disturbances are so detailed and authentic as to entitle them to the most implicit credit. The eye- and ear-witnesses were persons of strong understandings and well cultivated minds, unmuddled by superstition, and in some instances rather skeptically inclined."[9]

The entire Wesley family ultimately concluded that the cause of the phenomena was supernatural. John considered it the work of the devil but today's readers will likely prefer Mrs. Wesley's explanation. She supposed that the disturbances portended the death of her brother, who was working abroad for the East India Company. This gentleman, having recently acquired a large fortune, had suddenly disappeared and was never heard from again.

Or was he?

A Confounding Castle

Moving forward to the opening of the 19th century, we have a tale of a spooky castle that seems made for telling on dark and stormy nights. It has, however, been well attested to by the men involved — the two principals being Councilor Hahn, a high ranking official in the Prussian government and Charles Kern, a cornet in a hussar regiment. [10]

---

[9] Clarke, Dr. Adam, *Memoirs of the Wesley Family*, Vol. 1, Tess, 1823, p. 245. [This quote has been translated into contemporary English by the author.]

[10] This case is taken from *Die Scherin von Prevorst* [The Seeress of Prevorst] by Dr. Justinus Kerner, 1842. Both

In November of 1806, these men were assigned to temporary duty at a castle in Upper Silesia.[11] They were alone in the castle except for three servants. Being old friends, they decided to occupy the same apartment. Councilor Hahn was a student of philosophy and a confirmed materialist. Writing in the third person, he submitted a lengthy report of the events, the larger portion of which is copied here:

"During the first days of their residence in the castle, the two friends amused their long evenings with the works of Schiller, of whom they were both great admirers. Three days had thus passed quietly away, when, about nine o'clock in the evening as they were sitting at the table in the middle of the room, their reading was interrupted by a small shower of lime, which fell around them. They examined the ceiling, but could perceive no signs of it having fallen thence. As they were conversing of this, still larger pieces of lime fell around them. This lime was cold to the touch, as if detached from an outside wall.

"They finally set it down to the account of the old walls of the castle, and went to bed and to sleep. The next morning they were astonished at the quantity of lime that covered the floor, the more so as they could

---

Mrs. Crowe's and Mr. Owen's translations have been relied upon.

[11] An area that is now part of Poland.

not perceive on walls or ceiling the slightest appearance of injury. By evening, however, the incident was forgotten, until not only the same phenomenon recurred, but bits of lime were thrown about the room, several of which struck Hahn. At the same time loud knockings, like the reports of distant artillery, were heard, sometimes as if on the floor, sometimes as if on the ceiling. Again the friends went to bed; but the loudness of the knocks prevented their sleeping.

"Kern accused Hahn of causing the knockings by striking on the boards that formed the under portion of his bedstead, and was not convinced of the contrary till he had taken the light and examined for himself. Then Hahn conceived a similar suspicion of Kern. The dispute was settled by both rising and standing close together, during which time the knockings continued as before. Next evening, besides the throwing of lime and the knockings they heard another sound, resembling the distant beating of a drum.

"Thereupon they requested of a lady who had charge of the castle, Madame Knittel, the keys of the rooms above and below them; which she immediately sent them by her son. Hahn remained in the chamber below, while Kern and young Knittel went to examine the apartments in question. Above they found an empty room, below a kitchen. They knocked; but the sounds were entirely different from those that they had heard, and which Hahn at that very time continued to hear, in the room below. When they returned from their search, Hahn said, jestingly, 'The place is haunted.'

"They again went to bed, leaving the candles burning; but things became still more serious, for they distinctly heard a sound as if someone with loose slippers on was walking across the room; and this was accompanied also with a noise as of a walking-stick on which someone was leaning, striking the floor step by step; the person seeming, as far as one could judge by the sound, to be walking up and down the room. Hahn jested at this, Kern laughed, and both went to sleep, still not seriously disposed to ascribe these strange phenomena to any supernatural source.

"Next evening, however, it seemed impossible to ascribe the occurrences to any natural cause. The agency, whatever it was, began to throw various articles about the room; knives, forks, brushes, caps, slippers, padlocks, a funnel, snuffers, soap, in short, whatever was loose about the apartment. Even candlesticks flew about, first from one corner, then from another. If the things had been left lying as they fell, the whole room would have been strewed in utter confusion. At the same time, there fell, at intervals, more lime; but the knockings were discontinued. Then the friends called up the two coachmen and Hahn's servant, besides young Knittel, the watchman of the castle, and others; all of whom were witnesses of these disturbances. ...

"From the table, under their very eyes, snuffers and knives would occasionally rise, remain some time in the air, and then fall to the floor. In this way a large pair of scissors belonging to Hahn fell between him and one of the coachmen, and remained sticking in the floor.

"For a few nights it intermitted, then recommenced as before. After it had continued about three weeks, (during all which time Hahn persisted in remaining in the same apartment) tired out, at length, with the noises which continually broke their rest, the two friends resolved to have their beds removed into the corner room above, so as to obtain, if possible, a quiet night's sleep. But the change was unavailing. The same loud knockings followed them; and they even remarked that articles were flung about the room which they were quite certain they had left in the chamber below. ...

"A month had passed; the story of these disturbances had spread over the neighborhood, and had been received by many with incredulity; among the rest, by two Bavarian officers of dragoons, named Cornet and Magerle. The latter proffered to remain alone in the room; so the others left him there about twilight. But they had been but a short time in the opposite room, when they heard Magerle swearing loudly, and also sounds as of saber-blows on tables and chairs. So, for the sake of the furniture at least, they judged it prudent to look in upon Magerle. When they asked him what was the matter, he replied, in a fury, 'As soon as you left, the cursed thing began pelting me with lime and other things. I looked everywhere, but could see nobody; so I got in a rage, and cut with my saber right and left.'

"The party now passed the rest of the evening together in the room; and the two Bavarians closely watched Hann and Kern, in order to satisfy themselves that the mystery was no trick of theirs. All at once, as they were quietly sitting at the table, the snuffers rose into the air, and fell again to the ground behind Magerle; and a leaden ball flew at Hahn and hit him upon the chest. Presently afterwards, they heard a noise at the glass door, as if somebody had struck his fist through it, together with a sound of falling glass. On investigation, they found the door intact, but a broken drinking glass was on the floor. By this time the Bavarians were convinced, and they retired from the room to seek repose in one more peaceful. ...

"Hahn resolved that he would investigate them seriously. He accordingly, one evening, sat down at his writing table, with two lighted candles before him; being so placed that he could observe the whole room, and especially all the windows and doors. He was left, for a time, entirely alone in the castle, the coachmen being in the stables, and Kern having gone out. Yet the very same occurrences took place as before; nay, the snuffers, under his very eyes, were raised and whirled about. He kept the strictest watch on the doors and windows; but nothing could be discovered. ...

"The Chief Ranger, Radezensky, spent a night in the room; but although the two friends slept, he could get no rest. He was bombarded without intermission and, in the morning, his bed was found full of all manner of household articles. ...

"Inspector Knetch, from Koschentin, resolved to spend a night with Hahn and Kern. There was no end of the peltings they had during the evening; but finally they retired to rest, leaving the candles burning. Then all three saw two table-napkins rise to the ceiling in the middle of the room, there spread themselves out, and finally drop, fluttering, to the floor. A porcelain pipe bowl, belonging to Kern, flew around and broke to pieces. Knives and forks flew about; a knife fell on Hahn's head, striking him, however, with the handle only.

"Thereupon it was resolved, as these disturbances had now continued throughout two months, to move out of the room. Kern and Hahn's servant carried a bed into the opposite chamber. No sooner had they gone, than a water bottle that was standing in the room moved close to the feet of the two who remained behind. A brass candlestick also, that appeared to come out of a corner of the room, fell to the ground, before them. In the room to which they removed, they spent a

tolerably quiet night, though they could still hear noises in the room they had left. This was the last disturbance. …

"The story remained a mystery. All reflection on
these strange occurrences, all investigation, though
most carefully made, to discover natural causes for
them, left the observers in darkness. No one could
suggest any possible means of effecting them, even had
there been, which there was not, in the village or the
neighborhood, any one capable of sleight of hand. And
what motive could there be? The old castle was worth
nothing, except to its owner. In short, one can perceive
no imaginable purpose in the whole affair. It resulted
but in the disturbing of some men, and in the frightening of others; but the occupants of the room became,
during the two entire months that the occurrence lasted, as much accustomed to them as one can become to
any daily recurring annoyance."

The above narrative is subscribed and attested by
Hahn as follows: "I saw and heard every thing, exactly
as here set down; observing the whole carefully and
quietly. I experienced no fear whatever; yet I am whol-
ly unable to account for the occurrences narrated.

"Written this 19th of November, 1808 — Councilor
Hahn"

The Troublesome Tenant

Jumping forward nearly three decades, we briefly consider an unusually spirited relationship between a tenant and his landlord. In May of 1835, a Captain Molesworth rented one side of a duplex home from a Mr. Webster, who resided in the adjoining half. This was in Trinity, two miles from Edinburgh, Scotland.

Within two months of he and his daughter moving in, the captain began to hear noises that, he believed, must be coming from Mr. Webster's side of the home. His landlord denied these complaints, saying he certainly wouldn't do anything that might damage the reputation of his own house, or drive a responsible tenant out of it; and retorted that Molesworth must be causing the strange noises.

Meanwhile the disturbances continued both day and night. Sometimes there was the sound as of invisible feet; sometimes there were knockings, scratchings, or rustlings, first on one side, then on the other. Occasionally the unseen agent seemed to be rapping to a certain tune, and would answer, by so many knocks, any question to which the reply was in numbers; as, "How many persons are there in this room?"

So forcible at times were the poundings that the wall trembled visibly. Beds, too, were occasionally heaved up, as by some person underneath. Yet, search as they would, no perpetrator could be discovered. Captain Molesworth had the floorboards removed in the rooms where the noises were loudest and most frequent, and perforated the wall that divided his residence from Mr. Webster's; but without the least result.

Sheriff's officers, masons, justices of the peace, and the officers of the regiment quartered at Leith, all came to Molesworth's aid, in hopes of detecting or frightening away his tormentor; but in vain. Suspecting that it might be someone outside the house, they formed a cordon round it; but caught no intruder.

Finally fed-up with the constant disturbance, the landlord sued the tenant for damages to the property's reputation as well as for the lifted floorboards and the holes in the walls, not to mention the time that the captain fired a bullet into the wainscoting in a frustrated attempt to shoot the spirit. At the trial, all of the above facts, and more, were elicited by the plaintiff's attorney, who spent several hours in examining numerous witnesses. The published details of this case are based on the testimony of this attorney, a Scottish solicitor named Maurice Lothian.[12] The trial dragged on for at least two years, and apparently was never settled to anyone's satisfaction.

Once Molesworth moved from the premises, the commotion ceased. Soon afterward his daughter, who had been ill for some time, passed on.

---

[12] Later, Lothian became the Procurator Fiscal of the county of Edinburg.

Chapter Three

… Who's There? …

Everything of which we are ignorant appears improbable, but the improbabilities of today are the elementary truths of tomorrow.

— Charles Richet[13]

The four poltergeist cases presented in the previous chapter are just the tip of the iceberg, for there are records of scores of such cases prior to the mid-19th century, and hundreds up to the current time. In many, if not most, of these incidents, rappings, knockings, drumming, or similar percussive sounds are heard. And in more than a few, as in three of the four given above, these knocks have demonstrated sufficient awareness and intelligence to understand queries and provide correct answers. At Tedworth, the mysterious drum beats would mimic raps made by observers and sometimes seemed to play requested pieces. The Wesley family received several intelligent responses to both their verbal requests and their own knocks. And whatever was disturbing Captain Moles-

---

[13] *30 Years of Psychic Research*, p. 9.

worth's domicile would answer any question "to which the reply was in numbers."

Testing the Spirit

Despite the evidence that, in almost every case, some sort of intelligence was responsible for the disturbances, no one took the next step — and from our vantage point, the obvious step — and actually asked the "spirit" who it was. That didn't happen until 13 years after Molesworth's troubles began and an ocean away, in the small village of Hydesville, New York. And it only occurred then because a nine-year-old-girl's curiosity and verve overcame her natural fear of the unknown.

This child was one of two daughters living with their parents in a rented house while their new home was being built nearby. The year was 1848, the girl's name was Catherine (Kate) Fox, and this is her family's story:[14]

The Fox family were reputable farmers, members in good standing of the Methodist Church, and much respected by their neighbors as honest, upright people. Mr. John D. Fox was born in America of German descent. Mrs. Margaret Fox's ancestors were French and there was some history of psychic powers on her

---

[14] Much of this text comes from the works of the Hon. Robert Dale Owen and Sir Arthur Conan Doyle.

mother's side of the family. Mr. and Mrs. Fox had six children, of whom the two youngest — Margaret, twelve years old, and Kate, nine — were residing with them when, on the 11th of December, 1847, they moved into their temporary quarters.

Soon after their arrival, they began hearing many strange noises; but they assumed that rats and mice were the source. During the next month, however, the noises began to assume the character of slight knockings heard at night in the bedroom; sometimes appearing to sound from the cellar beneath. At first, Mrs. Fox sought to persuade herself this might be but the hammering of a shoemaker, in a house close by, sitting up late at work. But further observation showed that the sounds originated within the house For not only did the knockings gradually become more distinct, and not only were they heard first in one part of the house, then in another, but the family noticed that these raps, even when not very loud, often caused a motion, tremulous rather than a sudden jar, of the bedsteads and chairs, and sometimes of the floor. This motion was quite perceptible to the touch when a hand was laid on the chairs, was sometimes felt at night in the slightly oscillating motion of a bed, and was occasionally perceived as a sort of vibration when standing on the floor.

Toward the end of March, the disturbances increased in loudness and frequency. Mr. Fox and his wife got up night after night and thoroughly searched the house; but they discovered nothing. When the raps came on a door, Mr. Fox would stand, ready to open, the moment they were repeated. But this expedient, too, proved unavailing. Though he opened the door on the instant, there was no one to be seen. Next, he stationed himself outside of the door while his wife stood inside; but the knocks were heard on the door between them.

The only circumstance which seemed to suggest the possibility of trickery or of mistake was that these various incidents never happened in daylight. And thus, notwithstanding the strangeness of the thing, when morning came they began to think it must have been but the fancy of the night. Not being given to superstition, they clung, throughout several weeks of annoyance, to the idea that some natural explanation would at last appear. They did not abandon this hope until the night of Friday, the 31st of March, 1848.

The day had been cold and stormy, with snow on the ground. In the course of the afternoon, their son David came to visit them from his farm, about three miles distant. His mother then first recounted to him the particulars of the annoyances they had endured; for until now they had been little disposed to communicate these to anyone. He heard her with a smile. "Well, mother," he said, "I advise you not to say a word to the neighbors about it. When you find it out, it will be one of the simplest things in the world." And in that belief he returned home.

Wearied by a succession of sleepless nights and of fruitless attempts to penetrate the mystery, the Fox family retired very early on that Friday evening, hoping for a respite from the disturbances that harassed them. But they were doomed to disappointment.

The parents had moved the children's beds into their bedroom, but scarcely had the mother seen her daughters safely beneath the blankets, and was retiring herself, when the children cried out, "Here they are again!" Their mother chided them, and lay down. At which point the noises became louder and more startling. The children sat up in bed. Mrs. Fox called in her husband. The night being windy, he thought it might be the rattling of the sashes. He tried several, shaking them to see if they were loose. It was then that Kate pointed out that as often as her father shook a window sash the noises seemed to reply. Being a lively child, and in a measure accustomed to what was going on, she turned to where the noise was, snapped her fingers, and called out, "Here, old Splitfoot, do as I do!" The knocking instantly responded.

Others, as we have seen, had also noticed that their noisy ghosts would sometimes follow their lead and rap responses to their own raps, but Kate Fox next went where no man, or girl, had gone before — she raised her hand and moved her finger across her thumb in a snapping motion but she made no sound. Immediately a knock was sounded to this "silent snap." Clearly the maker of the noises could observe what was happening in the room! Kate called her mother's attention to this phenomenon. And as often as she repeated the noiseless motion, just so often responded the raps.

This at once arrested her mother's attention. "Count ten," she said, addressing the noise. Ten strokes, distinctly given! "How old is my daughter Margaret?" Twelve strokes! "And Kate?" Nine! "What can all this mean?" was Mrs. Fox's thought. Who was answering her? Was it only some mysterious echo of her own thought? But the next question which she put seemed to refute that idea. How many children have I?" she asked, aloud. Seven strokes. "Ah!" she thought, "it can blunder sometimes." And then, aloud, "Try again!" Still the number of raps was seven. But then she remembered something. "Are they all alive?" she asked. Silence, for answer. "How many are living?" Six strokes. "How many dead?" A single stroke. She had lost a child.

Then she asked, "Are you a man?" No answer. "Are you a spirit?" It rapped. "May my neighbors hear if I call them?" It rapped again.

Neighborly Ingenuity

Thereupon she asked her husband to call a neighbor, a Mrs. Redfield, who came in laughing. But her attitude was soon changed. The answers to her inquiries were as prompt and pertinent as they had been to those of Mrs. Fox. She was struck with awe; and when, in reply to a question about the number of her children, by rapping four, instead of three as she expected, it reminded her of a little daughter, Mary, whom she had recently lost, the mother burst into tears.

Other neighbors, attracted by the rumor of the disturbances, gradually gathered in, until the house was crammed with folks. Mrs. Fox left for the home of Mrs. Redfield, and the children were taken home by another neighbor. Mr. Fox remained in the crowded home.

Having formed a sort of informal committee of investigation, the crowd, in shrewd Yankee fashion, spent a large part of the night probing for information. They began to question the rapper using a "twenty questions" methodology wherein a response signified "yes" and the lack of a response meant "no."To ensure accuracy, each question was repeated in a reversed manner. For example, if the query "Were you a man?" received a positive response, the next question would be "Were you a woman?" And each time, the answer was properly the opposite of the initial response.

In this way the sounds alleged that they were produced by a spirit; by an injured spirit; by a spirit who had been murdered in that house; between four and five years ago; not by any of the neighbors (whose names were called over one by one) but by a former resident of the house, a certain John C. Bell, a blacksmith. His name was obtained by naming in succession the former occupants of the house.

The spirit alleged, further, that he had been murdered, at the age of 31, in the bedroom, for money, on a Tuesday night, at twelve o'clock; that no one but the murdered man and Mr. Bell were in the house at the time; that the body was carried down to the cellar early next morning, not through the outside cellar door, but by being dragged through the parlor into the pantry and thence down the cellar stairs; that it was buried, 10-feet deep, in the cellar, but not until the night after the murder.

Thereupon the assembled party adjourned to the cellar, which had an earthen floor. Mr. Redfield stood in various places and asked, each time, if that was the spot of burial. There was no response until he stood in the center. Then the noises were heard, as from beneath the ground. This was repeated several times, always with a similar result, no sound occurring when he stood at any other place than the center. One of the witnesses describes the sounds in the cellar as resembling "a thumping a foot or two under ground."

To double check this burial spot, on the following evening a group went into the cellar and all but one stood motionless while one person, Mr. Carlos Hyde, moved about to different spots. While this was going on, another neighbor, Mr. William Duesler, sat in the bedroom above and kept repeating the question: "Is anybody standing over the place where the body was buried?" In every instance, as soon as Mr. Hyde stepped to the center of the cellar the raps were sounded loudly enough to be heard in both the bedroom and the basement; but as often as he stood anywhere else, there was silence.

Although we have no record of who thought up the idea, it was also Duesler who, on that first night, sought to obtain information that could not be determined by single yes-or-no answers: the identity of the murdered man. He did that by calling out the letters of the alphabet, asking, at each, if that was the initial of the murdered man's first name; and so of the second name. The sounds responded at C and B. An attempt to obtain the entire name did not then succeed. At a later period the name "Charles B. Rosma" was given in the same way in reply to queries from David Fox.

It took four months of such tedious questioning before it was thought to ask the spirit to spell out answers by rapping once for the letter A, twice for B, thrice for C, etc. rather than having the questioner go through the alphabet over and over. Mr. Isaac Post will forever hold an honored place in the history of spirit communications because he made that suggestion.

The report of the night's wonders at Hydesville spread all over the neighborhood and beyond. On Saturday, the house was beset by a crowd of the curious. That night there were some three hundred people in and about the house. Various persons asked questions; and the replies corresponded at every point to those formerly given.

Then it was proposed to dig in the cellar; but, as the house stands on a flat plain not far from a small sluggish stream, the diggers reached water at the depth of less than three feet, and had to abandon the attempt. In the summer of 1848, when the water level was much lower, David Fox, Henry Bush, Lyman Granger, and others, recommenced digging in the cellar. At the depth of five feet they came to a plank, through which they bored with an auger, when, the auger-bit being loose, it dropped through out of sight. Digging further, they found several pieces of crockery and some charcoal and quicklime, indicating that the soil must at some time have been disturbed to a considerable depth; and finally they came upon some human hair and several bones, which proved to be portions of a human skeleton, including two bones of the hand and certain parts of the skull. But they found no corpse.

Supporting Testimony

Within a few weeks of the March 31st disturbances, a 40-page pamphlet[15] was published in which many of the neighbors gave testimony as to what they had witnessed.

Duesler stated that he inhabited the same house seven years before, and that during the term of his residence there he never heard any noise of the kind in or about the premises. He added that no other residents prior to Bell had any such experiences either. Apparently, the same cannot be said for the Bells themselves, for a near neighbor, Mrs. Pulver, claimed that Mrs. Bell once complained of not having slept at all during the previous night because she seemed to hear someone walking about from one room to another. Pulver further deposed that she heard Bell, on subsequent occasions, speak of unexplained noises.

Pulver's daughter, Lucretia, stated that she worked for and boarded with the Bells for three months during the winter of 1843-44 (which would have encompassed the time that the peddler claimed to have been murdered). She was 15-years old then and

---

[15] *A Report of the Mysterious Noises heard in the house of Mr. John D. Fox, in Hydesville, Arcadia, Wayne County, authenticated by the certificates and confirmed by the statements of that place and vicinity*, E.E. Lewis Publishers, Canandaigua, New York, 1848.

going to school. She stated that the Bells "appeared to be very good folks, only rather quick-tempered." Furthermore, she recalled that one afternoon a peddler, apparently about thirty years of age and having with him a trunk and a basket, called at the Bell's. Mrs. Bell informed Lucretia that she had known him formerly. Shortly after he came in, Mr. and Mrs. Bell consulted together for nearly half an hour in the pantry. Then Mrs. Bell told Lucretia — very unexpectedly to her — that they did not require her anymore; that she was going that afternoon to Lock Berlin,[16] and that Lucretia had better return home. Accordingly, Mrs. Bell and Lucretia left the house, the peddler and Mr. Bell remaining. Before she went, however, Lucretia looked at a piece of delaine[17] and told the peddler she would take enough to make a dress from it if he would call the next day at her father's house, which was nearby. He promised to do so, but he never showed up. In fact, none of the villagers could recall seeing the peddler since that time. Three days after she had left, Mrs. Bell returned and, to Lucretia's surprise, sent for her again to stay with them.

A few days after this, Lueretia began to hear knockings in her bedroom. The sounds seemed to be

---

[16] A town about seven miles east of Hydesville.

[17] Delaine is a light all-wool cloth of plain weave, usually printed.

under the foot of the bed, and were repeated during a number of nights. One night, when Mr. and Mrs. Bell had gone to Lock Berlin, and she had remained in the house, she heard footsteps. It sounded as if someone crossed the pantry, then went down the cellar stairs, then walked part of the way across the cellar, and stopped. About a week after this, Lucretia, having occasion to go down into the cellar, fell down near the middle of it. Mrs. Bell heard her yell and, when she came upstairs again, asked what was the matter. Lucretia exclaimed, "What has Mr. Bell been doing in the cellar?" Mrs. Bell replied that the soil must have been soften by rats. A few days afterward, at nightfall, Mr. Bell carried some earth into the cellar, and was at work there some time. Mrs. Bell said he was filling up the rat holes.

A couple that occupied the house for 18 months after the Bells moved out, Mr. and Mrs. Weekman, deposed that, one night as they were going to bed they heard knockings on the outside door; but when they opened there was no one there. This was repeated, until Mr. Weekman lost patience; and, after searching all round the house, he resolved, if possible, to detect these disturbers of his peace. Accordingly, he stood with his hand on the door, ready to open it at the instant the knocking was repeated. It was repeated, so that he felt the door jar under his hand; but, though he sprang out instantly and searched all round the house, he found not a trace of any intruder. From then on until they moved out, they were frequently disturbed by strange and unaccountable noises. One night Mrs. Weekman heard what seemed the footsteps of someone walking in the cellar.

As for Mr. Bell, he had moved to the town of Lyons, in the same county. On hearing the reports of the events, he showed up at his former residence, and got several of his prior neighbors to sign a certificate setting forth that "they never knew anything against his character." Of course, most of the worst serial killers of the past century would have been able to elicit similar testimony from their neighbors, prior to the exposure of their crimes. Bell's statement is dated only six days after the initial communications and weeks before the publication of most of the damning testimony. No charges were ever brought against Bell, however. And, apparently, no official ever asked him any hard questions, such as: "What was the name of the peddler with whom you were so friendly and where is he now?" and "Why did you let Lucretia go and then re-hire her three days later?"

Not every "statement" made via the raps could be verified. No record of a Charles B. Rosma could be located, despite the claim that the peddler had five children living in New York. And, most significantly, no skeleton was found in the cellar.

Bones Revealed

That is, no skeleton was found in the cellar until 56 years had passed. In November of 1904, children playing in what had become known as the "Spook House" noticed bones that led to the discovery of an entire skeleton buried between the earth and the crumbling cellar walls.[18] A tin "peddler's box" was found alongside the remains.

Although absolute certainty is impossible at this point in time, it's a good bet that John Bell did murder the peddler for his money (supposedly a substantial amount) and buried him quickly in the center of his cellar. Because of his haste and the high water table, the grave was likely shallow. Yes, the rappings said it was 10-feet deep, but a just deceased spirit cannot be expected to have an accurate sense of physical distance. Fearing that the hasty burial would be discovered, Bell very likely dug up the corpse a day or two later and re-interred it behind a cellar wall. This double digging would explain the soil being so soft that a young girl would sink into it.

And why, the reader might wonder, didn't the spirit of the peddler inform the citizens of Hydesville of his final resting place? Perhaps because no one asked. Once the inquisitors had ascertained that the body had been buried in the cellar (which it had been),

---

[18] *Boston Journal*, November 22, 1904, quoted by Doyle, p. 73.

they wouldn't have thought to ask if it had been later disinterred and buried elsewhere. And when Carlos Hyde walked about the space, William Duesler, in the room above, kept asking if anyone was standing "where the body was buried"? He didn't ask about where the body might have been sealed in a wall. Before discounting such an argument, consider the difficulty of inserting an entirely new line of thinking into a game of Twenty Questions. The spirit could only indicate yes or no, it had no way to say "Yes, but ..." or "Well, maybe ..." so how could it communicate that "yes" it had been buried in a certain spot, but "no" the body was no longer there?

Another possible reason for the spirit's failure to fully inform is that it simply didn't know that its body had been moved. The act of leaving your body doesn't make you omniscient. After the trauma of being murdered and the experience of watching his physical remains being buried in the dirt, it would be perfectly understandable if the peddler's soul abandoned the locale for a while and never witnessed the morbid resettlement of his bones.

Word Spreads

The Hydesville disturbances caught the attention of the entire country and, in a short time, of Europe as well. It is the seminal event in the history of Spiritualism. What made this event exceptional certainly was not any of the rather mundane messages received from beyond, nor the level of proof of an afterlife provided; rather, as Sir Arthur Conan Doyle has so well explained, its impact was so great because it "occurred within the ken of a practical people who found means to explore it thoroughly and to introduce reason and system into what had been a mere object of aimless wonder."

Of course, many people wondered why the spirit world would elect a murdered peddler as the herald of this new religion and why a backwater hamlet like Hydesville was chosen as the venue. One of the earliest psychical researchers of high-standing, Robert Hare, M.D., actually asked those questions during a séance. He was told "that the spirit of a murdered man would excite more interest, and that a neighbourhood was chosen where spiritual agency would be more readily credited than in more learned or fashionable and conspicuous circles, where the prejudice against supernatural agencies is extremely strong; but that the manifestations had likewise been made at Stratford, in Connecticut, under other circumstances. Nor were these the only places. They had been made elsewhere, without much success in awakening public attention."[19]

---

[19] Hare, Robert, *Experimental Investigation of the Spirit Manifestations*, Partridge & Brittan, 1855, p. 85.

As for the evidence that the events in Hydesville provide for Survival: there is the fact that something unseen was capable of observing and affecting the environs of the house. The pivotal issue with poltergeist activity is the possibility that the disturbances are actually telekinetic effects, generally unconscious, of a living person (usually a pubescent girl or boy). To those who are unfamiliar with the facts, the Fox sisters seem likely sources for such energies. But the knockings were heard in the house by the Weekmans and Lucretia Pulver long before Kate and Margaret came on the scene. Also, at the time that the crowd was asking questions in the cellar, the girls had been sent to stay with a neighbor. Therefore, those who would explain the case in terms of unconscious forces from living minds must posit at least four different people as sources — a far more incredible explanation than the survival of the peddler's spirit.

Nevertheless, to be truly convincing, the evidence should include the transmission of information from the supposed spirit to the living — information that the living would have no way of knowing otherwise. In this case, there is the information that a peddler was murdered by John Bell in the house; but all the physical evidence and testimony does not totally confirm that information.

And so, the evidence from the Hydesville case is strongly suggestive of Survival, but not absolute. If it stood alone, it would convince few people. As we have seen, though, it does not stand alone. It was preceded by numerous similar cases and, because this case received such fame, it was followed by a veritable explosion of spirit communications as the public woke up to their psychic potential.

Even though the citizens of Hydesville had never read the books of arcane history that told of disturbances at Tedworth, Epworth, Silesia, Edinburgh, and scores of other disturbed places, they applied their famous Yankee ingenuity and practical sense in examining the phenomena clearly and extracting the real meaning behind the spectacle. Because of their groundbreaking efforts, common folks throughout the world have learned that it is indeed possible to communicate directly with departed souls. The Fox family and their neighbors should forever be honored for their key role in reconnecting physical man with his spiritual essence.

Chapter Four

... The Alien Rapper!

There are no miracles that violate the laws of nature. There are only events that violate our limited knowledge of the laws of nature.

— St. Augustine

The Fox Family case clearly is key to the development of spirit communications throughout the ensuing century and a half. Of course, if little Kate Fox had not triggered it all with her silent mimicking of finger-snaps, sooner or later someone else would likely have taken her place in history. But it was Kate, and so a 9-year-old girl gets the credit for shaking up the world. It is fitting then, that 126 years later, another little girl became the central figure in the next major development of spirit-rap dialogue.

Like Kate Fox, Theresa Andrews was one of six children and shared a bedroom with an older sister in a rented house. At the time the knockings started, on 12 April 1974, Theresa was three years older than Kate was (in 1848) and the Andrews' home was in the Andover suburb of London rather than upstate New York.

The girls' bedroom was upstairs and shared a wall with an adjoining house. It was within this wall that the initial knocks were heard. Naturally, Theresa and her 20-year-old sister, Maria, first thought that the sounds were being made by their neighbors. They soon abandoned that idea, however, because they found that the knocks responded to Theresa's questions, even when she whispered the questions so softly that Maria could barely hear them from the adjacent bed.

The knocking usually began as the girls were about to sleep and seemed to be centered mostly around Theresa, although it sometimes occurred when no one was in the room. Soon, the girls developed a code in which one knock meant yes, two meant no, and three meant that the answer was unknown. It only took a few days before the code had been enhanced so that letters could be indicated by a number of raps indicating their position in the alphabet. Via this method, the rapper communicated that his name was Eric Waters. Despite never having experienced such events, nor even hearing of such things, the Andrews' family all took part in the questioning as if it were a game. The source of the sounds remained mysterious, but there seemed nothing sinister about the messages. At least at first.

Others, including neighbors, clergy, and police, were shortly called in to witness the events. All of them heard the raps but none could explain their origin. A woman claiming to have psychic powers visited the home and declared that the raps were caused by the spirit of a young boy who was murdered in the house and whose body was buried under the floorboards. (We are not told if this woman was familiar with the tale of the peddler in the cellar of the Fox home.) This revelation bothered the family and their discomfort seemed to infect Eric,[20] for the sessions became more erratic afterwards. Then, about 6:30 in the evening on April 29th, the knocking became unusually loud and continued far into the night despite the family's pleas for it to stop.

The next day, Barrie Colvin, an investigator who had conducted one prior interview with the family, was called back to the house in the hopes that he might find a means to bring an end to the disturbances. Altogether, Colvin visited the Andrew's household nine times, the last being on the 10th of June. Sometimes there was more activity than others. On one occasion, the banging was so loud and prolonged that, when Colvin arrived, a score of neighbors were gathered outside the Andrew's home listening to the racket, which could easily be heard from 50 yards down the street.

---

[20] For ease of reference, the source of the raps shall hereinafter be referred to by the name it claimed for itself.

During his investigations,[21] Colvin witnessed a number of intriguing performances by Eric. On the 2nd of May, at the suggestion of Colvin, Mrs. Andrews asked Eric to shift the location of his rapping from the wall to the headboard of Theresa's bed. Colvin reported the result thusly: "She then said: 'Eric, please try to knock on the headboard.' This was followed by a very soft tap, which was heard by us all. I was at that moment standing very close indeed to the headboard, with my ear about 15 cm from it. As Mrs. Andrews repeated the request, I put my hand on the headboard to see whether I could feel any sensation. Eric rapped progressively louder on the headboard and I could clearly feel the vibration. I noted, however, that on each occasion the onset of the vibration appeared to be slightly before the moment when we heard the rapping sound. (It is possible that this effect was purely subjective, but it felt real enough for me to make a note of it.)"[22]

Upon hearing that Theresa had discovered that Eric could correctly name whatever number she was thinking of, Colvin shuffled together four sets of cards

---

[21] Colvin, Barrie G., "The Andover Case: A Responsive Rapping Poltergeist," *Journal of the Society for Psychical Research*, Vol. 72.1, January 2008. This report was not published for 30 years at the request of the family involved. All family names are pseudonyms.

[22] *Ibid.*, p. 9.

numbered from 1 to 10. He picked a card at random, showed it to all in the room, and then held it facing the wall. When he asked Eric to rap the number on the card, Eric did so accurately. This test was run five times with the same correct results. Next, Colvin repeated the test, only without anyone but himself seeing the number prior to holding the card up to the wall. Out of a run of seven tries, Eric was correct each time. Then another run of ten tries and Eric was correct eight times and one number off two times. Lastly, for a run of ten tries, Colvin held the card to the wall without himself or anyone seeing it; Eric was correct eight times.[23] It's possible that the fewer people who were thinking of the number, the more difficulty Eric had ascertaining it; or it could simply be that, as he grew tired, Eric was less able to discern the number correctly.

Finally, Colvin attempted to gain some details about Eric's life. Many of his questions, though, were answered by the three knocks which signaled a lack of knowledge. Colvin reports, "Despite an apparent willingness to produce raps in reply to our questions, we were unable to find out much about Eric and concluded that he seemed to know very little about his life." To explain this lack, Colvin offers the explanation that Eric's manifestations are "derived from the mind of The-

---

[23]*Ibid.*, p. 12.

rcsa" and that "if she had a rather incomplete picture of Eric's family history, it was perhaps to be expected that Eric would be unable to formulate answers to some apparently simple questions."[24] I suggest that another explanation might better fit the facts.

Often during the rapping sessions, Eric would seem to get angry over minor things. At times he would get silly, giving responses just the opposite of what was requested. If he was slighted or ignored, Eric would suddenly go quiet, sometimes refusing to respond for several days. In short, Eric's actions were consistent with those of a child: sometimes sincere, sometimes needy, sometimes petulant. And while a child might be good at numbers or the alphabet, it's no surprise that he would have trouble with dates and the names of people and places from long ago.[25]

Whatever the truth about Eric's origins, he was unable to supply any useful information about his life and Colvin was unable to find any record of an Eric Waters ever residing in the Andover neighborhood. (Of course, Eric never claimed to be from that neighborhood.)

If that were the end of the tale, Theresa and Eric would be little more than curious footnotes in the lit-

---

[24] *Ibid.*, p. 13.

[25] In fact, the names of people are notoriously difficult for the spirits of adults to recall and/or communicate.

erature of the paranormal. Despite Eric's claims and his ability to see cards held against a wall, the case provides rather weak evidence for Survival.

The true value of this story did not become apparent until Colvin subjected recordings of the rapping and knocking sounds to analysis using modern acoustical-research tools. In April 2010, he published a 29-page report[26] of his tests on both the Andover rappings and several similar cases. The technicalities are far too complex to accurately relay here, so the following simplified synopsis will have to do. The simplicity of my explanation should not be allowed to lessen the great importance of the findings.

When one object is struck upon another – such as a knuckle upon a wall, a stick upon a board, or a hammer upon a gong – the sound wave will taper off differently depending upon the objects, but the wave always begins abruptly. For example, a bell will ring for some time after it is struck by its clapper, but before it is struck it makes no noise and when it is struck the sound produced is instantly as loud as it's going to get. That is, the sound wave reaches maximum amplitude immediately. The waveform in Figure 1 illustrates this characteristic.

---

[26] Colvin, Barrie G., "The Acoustic Properties of Unexplained Rapping Sounds," *Journal of the Society for Psychical Research*, Vol. 74.2, April 2010, pp. 65-93.

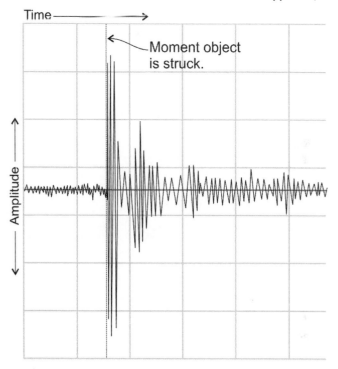

Figure 1. Typical waveform of normal rap.

This characteristic has been shown to hold no matter what the objects are, including knuckles on a wall, a spoon tapping a wine glass, and a rubber mallet striking a rubber mat.[27]

But waveform analysis of the recordings made of the Andover raps shows a marked difference: instead of reaching maximum amplitude immediately, the sound builds to a peak over time. See Figure 2.

---

[27] Colvin, *Acoustic*, pp. 72-73.

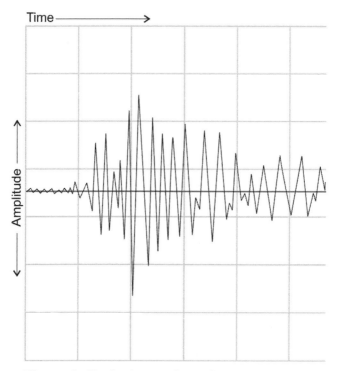

Figure 2. Typical waveform from Andover raps.

When Colvin noted that he seemed to feel a vibration in Theresa's headboard prior to hearing the knock, he was correct!

Other researchers have made similar observations and numerous recordings have been made by investigators of poltergeist phenomena, but the Andover case inspired Colvin to go a step or two further. He managed to obtain recordings of supposed paranormal sounds from ten separate cases that were investigated between 1960 and 2000. These he subjected to careful acoustical analysis, and, in every case, he discovered the same waveform patterns. Every rap known to be made by living humans reached maximum loudness instantly; every knock, rap, or bang of apparent paranormal origin exhibited a more gradual rise to maximum amplitude.

These ten cases were not picked because anyone thought they were the strongest or most evidential, but simply because they were the ones for which recordings were available. This means their selection for analysis was essentially random and indicates a high probability that most, if not all, similar claims of paranormal raps should be assumed true until proven otherwise. In other words, because ten cases selected essentially at random all displayed a common attribute, the odds are excellent that all well-documented cases will also share that attribute. If you were to reach blindly into a bag of marbles and pull out a blue one, you couldn't attach any meaning to it. But if you reach into the bag ten times in a row and get ten blue marbles, then you can be pretty sure that the remaining marbles are also blue. We can't be absolutely certain in every case, but it seems fair to assume that raps that exhibit this gradual rise to maximum amplitude indicate the exercise of physical powers that reside beyond the bounds of the material world.

[Note: Further research[28] has created the need to qualify this statement somewhat. Tests done by Roemer, *et. al.*, demonstrated that by placing the microphone on a solid surface a fair distance from the impact site, the immediate rise in amplitude could be softened enough to mimic the psi raps in a few cases. This effect is likely due to vibrations traveling through the floorboards, the walls, and the support structure prior to reaching the microphone. Thus, it would be more accurate to state that "<u>raps recorded via a microphone held in the vicinity of the apparent source </u>that exhibit this gradual rise to maximum amplitude indicate the exercise of physical powers that reside beyond the bounds of the material world."]

In the future, investigators might be able to save a great deal of time using this approach instead of spending hours peering behind doors and under tables. Likewise, we no longer have to suffer skeptics claims of hidden accomplices or popping toe joints. If acoustical analysis says the sounds aren't of incarnate origin, the argument should be settled.

Perhaps even more important to the human race is that Colvin seems to have developed convincing evidence, if not absolute proof, of the existence of a heretofore unknown source of energy. For decades we have been reading about the search for whatever it is that

[28] See the, *JSPR*. Vol. 75.1, pp. 61-63; and Vol. 75.3, p. 175.

powers UFOs, while all the time a truly alien energy source has been right under our noses, or inside our tables and walls. The topic is outside the scope of this book, but it is such an interesting concept that I couldn't help mentioning it.

To get back to the subject at hand … demonstrating that a sound was not made by any physical action does not prove that it was made by the dead, but it does demonstrate the existence of mental/spiritual powers capable of affecting our physical world. Replication of Colvin's work by other scientists is required, but these special waveforms certainly appear to qualify as what Alex Imich calls "The Crucial Demonstration" of the existence of paranormal phenomena.

Given the fact that some intelligence is proficient at discerning our actions, responding wisely and sometimes wittily to our questions, providing information unknown to us, and manipulating physical matter in ways we cannot, it seems both illogical and presumptuous of us to reject its claim of being an independent spirit who once lived on this earth.

Visions and Dreams

I start from the position that most people tell the truth as they believe it to be. It would be difficult to get through life if you took a different view. ... Even science would fall apart, because we can't all verify everything for ourselves. ... If a physicist wants to leave square one he has to rely on other people's eyewitness statements, and believe that the instrumental data they produce in support of their anecdotes are authentic.

— Mary Rose Barrington[29]

In this chapter, and in chapters 7, 9, 11, 13, and 15, you will find cases taken from the Survival Top 40 (see www.SurvivalTop40.com) and grouped by type. Citations of the source material for these cases can be found at the end of each chapter. The cases were ranked using the Evidence Scoring System, which is discussed in Appendix Three.

---

[29] "Broken Threads in the Fabric of Physical Reality," *The Paranormal Review*, October 2009, pp. 27-28.

The Wealthy Wall
[Case ID# 33, ESS Score = 255, Current Rank 38th]

A Houston businessman named Charles Vance experiences an unusually vivid and memorable dream in which he sees a man standing in front of a brightly painted cottage. He recognizes the man as a fellow named Murphy who, many years before, had been a mentor and father figure to Vance. After Vance married, he and his wife often visited Murphy and his wife, Lorraine; but the couples had drifted apart a few years before Murphy's death.

In the dream, Murphy says that it is important for Vance to tell Lorraine "to look in the hall — just south of the bedroom, to the right of the light socket — inside that wall." Vance tells his own wife of the dream, but refuses to call Lorraine, being sure that she would think him nuts. But the dream is repeated four or five times and, finally, Vance's wife, seeing how disturbed Vance is becoming, calls Lorraine herself and tells her about the dreams. Shortly, a very excited Lorraine calls back to say that she had broken into the wall indicated by her husband's spirit and found a cache of "thousands and thousands of dollars."

Lorraine also informed the Vances that her house was scheduled to be remodeled during the following week and the money might well have been found by one of the laborers. Of course, he might have turned it over to Lorraine, but perhaps not. Thus the urgency of

Murphy's message was most reasonable at that time. Lorraine claims that she had absolutely no idea that any money had been hidden in the house.

When Lorraine called her daughter in Florida to tell her about the fortunate discovery, the daughter replied that she had been having the same dreams as had Vance, but had ignored them. The woman was Murphy's step-daughter and the Vances had never met her.

This story was revealed, rather reluctantly, to its author after a friend had urged her to contact the Vances.

The Ramhurst Revenants
[Case ID# 25, ESS Score = 256, Current Rank 36th]

In 1866, Alfred Russel Wallace,[30] described this case as one in which the evidence for the appearance of spirits was "as good and definite as it is possible for any evidence of any fact to be." One hundred and thirty-three years later, author Susy Smith claimed it was her favorite ghost story.[31] The text here is taken from a book by Robert Dale Owen. A former member of the Indiana Constitutional Convention, a U.S. Congressman (drafter of the bill to establish the Smithsonian Institution) and an American Minister at Naples, Owen was the author of many works, including *The Policy of*

---

[30] *The Scientific Aspect of the Supernatural*, 1866, p. 21.

[31] Smith, Susy, *Life Is Forever*, toExcel Press, 1999, p.53.

Emancipation. He was an outspoken skeptic of paranormal events until he witnessed a few astounding phenomena for himself. He then set himself the task of collecting the best evidence for Survival available at the time.

Owen writes: "In October, 1857, and for several months afterwards, Mrs. Reynolds,[32] the wife of a field officer of high rank in the British army, was residing in Ramhurst Manor House, near Leigh, in Kent, England. From the time of her first occupying this ancient residence, every inmate of the house had been more or less disturbed at night — not usually during the day — by knockings and sounds as of footsteps, but more especially by voices, which could not be accounted for. These last were usually heard in some unoccupied adjoining room; sometimes as if talking in a loud tone, sometimes as if reading aloud, occasionally as if screaming. The servants were much alarmed. They never saw anything; but the cook told Mrs. Reynolds that on one occasion, in broad daylight, hearing the rustle of a silk dress close behind her, and which seemed to touch her, she turned suddenly round, supposing it to be her mistress, but, to her great surprise and terror, could see nobody. Mrs. Reynolds's brother,

---

[32] All names here are pseudonyms. Owen was personally acquainted with both "Reynolds" and "Stevens."

a bold, light-hearted young officer, fond of field-sports, and without the slightest faith in the reality of visitations from another world, was much disturbed and annoyed by these voices, which he declared must be those of his sister and of a lady friend of hers, sitting up together to chat all night. On two occasions, when a voice which he thought to resemble his sister's rose to a scream, as if imploring aid, he rushed from his room, at two or three o'clock in the morning, gun in hand, into his sister's bedroom, there to find her quietly asleep.

"On the second Saturday in the above month of October, Mrs Reynolds drove over to the railway-station at Tunbridge, to meet her friend Miss Stevens, whom she had invited to spend some weeks with her. This young lady had been in the habit of seeing apparitions, at times, from her early childhood.

"When, on their return, at about four o'clock in the afternoon, they drove up to the entrance of the manor-house, Miss Stevens perceived on the threshold two figures, apparently an elderly couple, habited in the costume of a former age. They appeared as if standing on the ground. She did not hear any voice; and, not wishing to render her friend uneasy, she made at that time no remark to her in connection with this apparition.

"She saw the appearance of the same figures, in the same dress, several times within the next ten days, sometimes in one of the rooms of the house, sometimes in one of the passages — always by daylight. They appeared to her surrounded by an atmosphere nearly of the color usually called neutral tint. On the third occasion they spoke to her, and stated that they had been husband and wife, that in former days they had possessed and occupied that manor-house, and that their name was Children. They appeared sad and downcast; and, when Miss Stevens inquired the cause of their melancholy, they replied that they had idolized this property of theirs; that their pride and pleasure had centered in its possession; that its improvement had engrossed their thoughts; and that it troubled them to know that it had passed away from their family and to see it now in the hands of careless strangers.

"I asked Miss Stevens how they spoke. She replied that the voice was audible to her as that of a human being's; and that she believed it was heard also by others in an adjoining room. This she inferred from the fact that she was afterward asked with whom she had been conversing.* [*Footnote in Owen's text:* * Yet this is not conclusive. It might have been Miss Steven's voice only that was heard, not any reply — though heard by her — made by the apparitions. Visible to her, they were invisible to others. Audible to her, they may to others have been inaudible also. Yet it is certain that the voices at night were heard equally by all.]

"After a week or two, Mrs. Reynolds, beginning to suspect that something unusual, connected with the constant disturbances in the house, had occurred to her friend, questioned her closely on the subject; and then Miss Stevens related to her what she had seen and heard, describing the appearances and relating the conversation of the figures calling themselves Mr. and Mrs. Children.

"Up to that time, Mrs. Reynolds, though her rest had been frequently broken by the noises in the house, and though she too has the occasional perception of apparitions, had seen nothing; nor did any thing appear to her for a month afterward. One day, however, about the end of that time, when she had ceased to expect any apparition to herself, she was hurriedly dressing for a late dinner, her brother, who had just returned from a day's shooting, having called to her in impatient tones that dinner was served and that he was quite famished. At the moment of completing her toilet, and as she hastily turned to leave her bed-chamber, not dreaming of any thing spiritual, there in the doorway stood the same female figure Miss Stevens had described — identical in appearance and costume, even to the old point-lace on her brocaded silk dress — while beside her, on the left, but less distinctly visible, was the figure of her husband. They uttered no sound; but above the figure of the lady, as if written in phosphoric light in the dusk atmosphere that surrounded her, were the words 'Dame Children,' together with some other words, intimating that, having never aspired beyond the joys and sorrows of this world, she had remained 'earth-bound.' These last, however, Mrs. Reynolds scarcely paused to decipher; for a renewed appeal from her brother, as to whether they were to have any dinner that day, urged her forward. The figure, filling up the doorway, remained stationary. There was no time for hesitation: she closed her eyes, rushed through the apparition and into the dining room, throwing up her hands and exclaiming to Miss Stevens, 'Oh, my dear, I've walked through Mrs. Children!'

"This was the only time during her residence in the old manor-house that Mrs. Reynolds witnessed the apparition of these figures.

"And it is to be remarked that her bed-chamber, at the time, was lighted, not only by candles, but by a cheerful fire, and that there was a lighted lamp in the corridor which communicated thence to the dining-room.

"This repetition of the word 'Children' caused the ladies to make inquiries among the servants and in the neighborhood whether any family bearing that name had ever occupied the manor-house. Among those whom they thought likely to know something about it was a Mrs. Sophy Osman, a nurse in the family, who had spent her life in that vicinity. But all inquiries were fruitless; every one to whom they put the question, the nurse included, declaring that they had never heard of such a name. So they gave up all hopes of being able to unravel the mystery.

"It so happened, however, that, about four months afterward, this nurse, going home for a holiday to her family at Riverhead, about a mile from Seven Oaks, and recollecting that one of her sisters-in-law, who lived near her, an old woman of seventy, had fifty years before been housemaid in a family then residing at Ramhurst, inquired of her if she had ever heard any thing of a family named Children. The sister-in-law replied that no such family occupied the manor-house when she was there; but she recollected to have then seen an old man who told her that in his boyhood he had assisted to keep the hounds of the Children family, who were then residing at Ramhurst. This information the nurse communicated to Mrs. Reynolds on her return; and thus it was that that lady was first informed that a family named Children really had once occupied the manor-house.

"All these particulars I received in December, 1858, directly from the ladies themselves, both being together at the time.

"Even up to this point the case, as it presented itself, was certainly a very remarkable one. But I resolved, if possible, to obtain further confirmation in the matter.

"I inquired of Miss Stevens whether the apparitions had communicated to her any additional particulars connected with the family. She replied that she recollected one which she had then received from them, namely, the husband's name was Richard. At a subsequent period likewise, she had obtained the date of Richard Children's death, which, as communicated to her, was 1753. She remembered also that on one occasion a third spirit appeared with them, which they stated was their son; but she did not get his name. To my further inquiries as to the costumes in which the (alleged) spirits appeared, Miss Stevens replied 'that they were of the period of Queen Anne or one of the early Georges, she could not be sure which, as the fashions in both were similar.' These were her exact words. Neither she nor Mrs. Reynolds, however, had obtained any information tending either to verify or to refute these particulars.

"Having an invitation from some friends residing near Seven Oaks, in Kent, to spend with them the Christmas week of 1858, I had a good opportunity of prosecuting my inquiries in the way of verification."

[At this point in his testimony, Owens relates how he visited the nurse, Sophy Osman, and she confirmed Reynold's story of strange voices, footsteps, and the incident with the cook hearing a silk dress rustle behind her. A nice corroboration, but we need to trim this tale somewhere.]

"But as all this afforded no clew either to the Christian name, or the date of occupation, or the year of Mr. Children's death, I visited, in search of these, the church and graveyard at Leigh, the nearest to the Ramhurst property, and the old church at Tunbridge; making inquiries in both places on the subject. But to no purpose. All I could learn was, that a certain George Children left, in the year 1718, a weekly gift of bread to the poor, and that a descendant of the family, also named George, dying some forty years ago, and not residing at Ramhurst, had a marble tablet, in the Tunbridge church, erected to his memory.

"Sextons and tombstones having failed me, a friend suggested that I might possibly obtain the information I sought by visiting a neighboring clergyman. I did so, and with the most fortunate result. Simply stating to him that I had taken the liberty to call in search of some particulars touching the early history of a Kentish family of the name of Children, he replied that, singular enough, he was in possession of a document, coming to him through a private source, and containing, he thought likely, the very details of which I was in search. He kindly intrusted it to me; and I found in it, among numerous particulars regarding another member of the family, not many years since de-

ccased, certain extracts from the 'Hasted Papers,' preserved in the British Museum; these being contained in
a letter addressed by one of the members of the Children family to Mr. Hasted. Of this document, which
may be consulted in the Museum library, I here tran-
scribe a portion, as follows:

> 'The family of Children were settled for a great
> many generations at a house called, from their
> own name, Childrens, situated at a place called
> Nether Street, otherwise Lower Street,
> Hildenborough, in the parish of Tunbridge.
> George Children of Lower Street, who was
> High~Sheriff of Kent in 1698, died without issue in
> 1718, and by will devised the bulk of his estate to
> Richard Children, eldest son of his late uncle, Wil-
> liam Children of Hedcorn, and his heirs. This
> Richard Children, *who settled himself at Ramhurst*,[33]
> in the parish of Leigh, married Anne, daughter of
> John Saxby, in the parish of Leeds, by whom he
> had issue four sons and two daughters, &c.'

"Thus I ascertained that the first of the Children
family who occupied Ramhurst as a residence was
named Richard, and that he settled there in the early
part of the reign of George I. The year of his death;
however, was not given.

---

[33] Emphasis is Owen's (I assume).

"This last particular I did not ascertain till several months afterward; when a friend versed in antiquarian lore, to whom I mentioned my desire to obtain it, suggested that the same Hasted, an extract from whose papers I have given, had published, in 1778, a history of Kent, and that, in that work, I might possibly obtain the information I sought. In effect, after considerable search, I there found the following paragraph:

> `In the eastern part of the Parish of Lyghe (now Leigh), near the river Medway, stands an ancient mansion called Ramhurst, once reputed a Manor and held of the honor of Gloucester." ... "It continued in the Culpepper family for several generations." ... "It passed by sale into that of Saxby, and Mr. William Saxby conveyed it, by sale, to Children. Richard Children, Esq., resided here, and died possessed of it in 1753, aged eighty-three years. He was succeeded in it by his eldest son, John Children, of Tunbridge, Esq., whose son, George Children, of Tunbridge, Esq., is the present possessor.'* [Footnote in Owen's text: *That is, in 1778, when the work was published. See, for the above quotation, *Hasted's History of Kent*, Vol. i, pp. 422 and 423.]

"Thus I verified the last remaining particular, the date of Richard Children's death. It appears from the above, also, that Richard Children was the only representative of the family who lived and died at Ramhurst; his son John being designated not as of Ramhurst, but as of Tunbridge. From the private memoir above referred to I had previously ascertained that the family seat after Richard's time was Ferox Hall, near Tunbridge.

"It remains to be added that in 1816, in consequence of events reflecting no discredit on the family, they lost all their property, and were compelled to sell Ramhurst, which has since been occupied, though a somewhat spacious mansion, not as a family residence, but as a farmhouse. I visited it; and the occupant assured me that nothing worse than rats or mice disturbs it now.

"I am not sure that I have found on record, among what are usually termed ghost-stories, any narrative better authenticated than the foregoing. It involves, indeed, no startling or romantic particulars, no warning of death, no disclosure of murder, no circumstances of terror or danger; but it is all the more reliable on that account; since those passions which are wont to excite and mislead the imaginations of men were not called into play.

"It was communicated to me, about fourteen months only after the events occurred, by both the chief witnesses, and incidentally confirmed, shortly afterward, by a third.

"The social position and personal character of the two ladies to whom the figures appeared preclude, at the outset, all idea whatever of willful misstatement or deception. The sights and sounds to which they testify did present themselves to their senses Whether their senses played them false is another question."

At this point, Mr. Owen begins his analysis of the case. He first points out that Miss Stevens first saw the figures, "not in the obscurity of night, not between sleeping and waking, not in some old chamber reputed to be haunted, but in the open air, and as she was descending from a carriage, in broad daylight." He mentions the numerous encounters, both visual and auditory, and the multiple witnesses. His major point, of course, is the precise information (names and dates) communicated by the spirits, information that was confirmed only later by his own research in obscure places.

Cloak & Danger
[Case ID# 44, ESS Score = 267, Current Rank 21st]

Vincent and Ivan Idanowicz lived in the house of their employer, Joseph Kronhelm. One November day in 1894, Vincent[34] traveled to the nearby town of

---

[34] I will use first names for ease of distinguishing between the brothers Idanowicz.

Gajsin seeking a new fur cloak to keep the Russian winters at bay. While he considered various fabrics in the shop of Izloma Sierota, the tailor brought out an almost new cloak that, he said, had belonged to a gentleman named Lassota. The low asking price of 45 rubles convinced Vincent to buy this cloak instead of ordering a new one, and he went home with his purchase, pleased with the bargain he had gotten.

That night, however, Vincent was awakened from a sound sleep by "a gentleman dressed in black." Even though the door to the bedroom was locked, and his brother slept undisturbed nearby, Vincent felt only surprise, not fear. The visitor warned Vincent to return the cloak immediately as it was infested with tuberculosis bacteria. The cloak had come, he said, from a judge who had recently died of TB, not from Mr. Lassota, as the tailor had claimed. And then, the visitor simply vanished.

Vincent woke up his brother, who only laughed at his story. And, since a careful check revealed no way that anyone could have entered the bedroom, Vincent came to accept that he had experienced a hallucination. He spoke not a word of the vision throughout the following day. That night, however, the visitor came again. This time, the brothers were discussing family matters when the man in black came banging through the door and said: "You are both awake. Well, this time, Mr. Vincent, you will not say that my appearance yesterday was a hallucination. I come, therefore, to re-peat to you: Go and ask Mr. Kronhelm to allow you to go to Gajsin tomorrow, and return the fur to Sierota, who is deceiving you in saying that it belonged to Mr. Lassota. I repeat that it belonged to a judge, who died of tuberculosis at Gajsin. It is infected with tuberculosis bacilli. I was a Government official at Lipowice, and died there in 1892; but as my mission is to watch over you, I warn you of what will happen if you do not fol-low my advice." So saying, the apparition vanished.

Kronhelm reports that he was awakened at 5:00 a.m. by two pale and frightened brothers. Upon hear-ing their story, he decided to accompany them to Gajsin.

When questioned by the three men, the tailor in-sisted that he had been truthful when he told Vincent that he had bought the cloak from a Mr. Lassota. So, the trio went to see the current judge at Gajsin, who confirmed that his predecessor had died of tuberculo-sis, but knew nothing about his effects. The judge di-rected them to a dealer in second-hand goods named Fonkonogy. This man told Kronhelm that he had bought all the effects of the late judge, except for a fur cloak, which had been bought by the tailor, Sierota. The men showed him the fur cloak and he recognized it at once. Later he signed a written affirmation of his testimony.

Written statements were also signed by both of the brothers and by the priest in attendance at the judge's death. What happened to the cloak, or to the tailor, was never reported.

The author of the article from which this case is derived, took a super-cautious approach that was typical of the early SPR members. In her attempts to offer explanations other than Survival, she repeatedly piles "might be's" on top of "could have's" on top of "may have's"; cobbling together arguments so unlikely and ungainly as to be laughable. An example of this is her suggestion that Vincent "may have" been in the habit of visiting Gajsin, and that the judge "may have" been pointed out to him, and "could have" been wearing the cloak, and it "might have" some identifying mark, that Vincient's subconscious mind "may have" registered and so "might have" recognized, and something in the tailor's manner "might have" seemed suspicious, and then, in response to all that, Vincent's subconscious "could have" created an elaborate dramatic presentation (i.e. the ghost). But even if every one of these assumptions were not completely unfounded, they fail to explain three things: (1) how Vincent's subconscious linked the cloak to tuberculosis, (2) why the ghost was of a complete stranger rather than the judge himself or someone Vincent trusted, and (3) how it was that brother Ivan saw and heard the same apparition.

Regarding the visitor's identity, Johnson points to the lack of verification of the name it gave and she suggests that the case is somehow weakened thereby. But spirits are known to adapt an image and name acceptable to their audience. Who they "really are" could well interfere with the reception of their message. If, for example, the spirit had admitted that he was a Hindu, or a Cherokee, or something equally outlandish to someone raised in the Greek Orthodox church, his warning would most likely have never been heeded.

Sources
Visions and Dreams

The Wealthy Wall
Arcangel, Dianne, *Afterlife Encounters*, Hampton Roads
    Publishing, 2005, pp. 74-82.

The Ramhurst Revenants
Owen, Robert Dale, *Footfalls On The Boundary Of Another
    World*, 1859, reprinted by Kessinger Publishing, pp. 414-
    427.

Cloak and Danger
Johnson, Alice, "A Case of Information Supernormally
    Acquired" *Proceedings of the Society for Psychical
    Research*, Vol. 12, 1897.

The Reticence of Scientists

It is unfortunate that learned men, who see the phenomena for the first time, commit the error of supposing that their entry into the arena marks the beginning of the proper investigation of mediumistic phenomena.
— Baron Albert von Schrenck-Notzing, M.D.[35]

Sooner or later, any student of psychic phenomena is bound to wonder why the scientific and academic communities are so reticent to investigate the subject. When scientists who have made disparaging remarks about psychic phenomena are asked what actual investigation they have done to reach such an opinion, their answer will not only be "none" but, more often than not, that answer will be expressed in a disdainful tone suggesting that any such effort would be a waste of their valuable time.

The ignorance these scientists thereby demonstrate is partly the fault of those researchers who have investigated and yet have been reticent in proclaiming the results of their investigations. Professor James

---

[35] von Schrenck-Notzing, Albert, *Phenomena of Materialisation*, E.P. Dutton & Co., 1923, p. 292.

Hyslop, PhD., LL.D., once wrote that most of the leading members of the Society for Psychical Research "who have conducted personal investigations have become convinced that man survives bodily death; but it has been regarded as not always good policy to avow the conviction with any missionary zeal. Hence, conviction on the point appears to the public to be less strong than it actually is."[36] If the experts are not pressuring academia to accept their conclusions, it's no surprise that scientists shy away from personal investigation, especially in light of what I call "conversion phobia."

Simply put, conversion phobia is the worry that if one opens oneself to a new idea, one might be forced to agree with it. And, in the case of Survival, the penalties for doing so can be severe. Scientists generally are not stupid. They know that the history of science is littered with the carcasses of their brothers who have felt compelled to investigate the afterlife with an open mind and report their findings honestly.

Scattered throughout this book are short "Conversion Phobia" sections containing quotes from a few of the scientists who were brave and honest enough to publicly admit their change of mind.

---

[36] Hyslop, James, *Contact With The Other World*, The Century Co., 1919, p. 35.

Robert Hare

In 1818, Hare was called to the chair of chemistry and natural philosophy at William and Mary and that same year was appointed as professor of chemistry in the department of medicine at the University of Pennsylvania, where he would remain until his retirement in 1847. He was awarded honorary M.D. degrees from Yale in 1806 and Harvard in 1816. In 1839, he was the first recipient of the Rumford Award for his invention of the oxy-hydrogen blow-pipe and his improvements in galvanic methods. He was a member of the American Academy of Arts and Sciences, the American Philosophical Society, and an honorary life member of the Smithsonian Institute.

In His Own Words:

"In common with almost all educated persons of the nineteenth century, I had been brought up deaf to any testimony which claimed assistance from supernatural causes, such as ghosts, magic, or witchcraft, [and] I was at that time utterly incredulous of any cause of the phenomena excepting unconscious muscular action on the part of the persons with whom the phenomena were associated."[37]

"I sincerely believe that I have communicated with the spirits of my parents, sister, brother, and dearest friends"[38]

"The most precise and laborious experiments which I have made in my investigation of Spiritualism, have been assailed by the most disparaging suggestions, as respects my capacity to avoid being the dupe of any medium employed. Had my conclusions been of the opposite kind, how much fulsome exaggeration had there been, founded on my experience as an investigator of science for more than half a century! And now, in a case when my own direct evidence is adduced, the most ridiculous surmises as to my probable oversight or indiscretion are suggested, as the means of escape from the only fair conclusion"[39]

---

[37] Hare, Robert, *Experimental Investigation of the Spirit Manifestations*, Partridge & Brittan, 1855, p. 37.

[38] *Ibid.*, p. 12.

[39] *Ibid.*, p. 13.

Chapter Six

Spontaneous Spirits

We are so far from knowing all the agents of nature and their various modes of action, that it would not be scientific to deny any phenomena merely because, in the current state of our knowledge, they are inexplicable.

— M. le Marquis de La Place[40]

We had just sat down in the anteroom to enjoy a cup of afternoon tea when he said:

"You know, we have spent considerable time examining reports of NDEs [Near Death Experiences] and we have spoken briefly of the NDA [Nearing Death Awareness] but we would be remiss if we didn't also pay some attention to those interactions with the spirit world that are unsought, unplanned, and unpredictable. Authors Bill and Judy Guggenheim[41] have named these 'After-Death Communications' (ADCs), and that name seems to be most popular. Author Diane

---

[40] *Théorie analytique des Probabilités,* p. 43.

[41] Guggenheim, Bill and Judy Guggenheim, *Hello From Heaven,* Bantam Books, 1995.

Arcangel[42] refers to them as 'Afterlife Encounters' (AEs). Personally, I prefer Spontaneous Trans-dimensional Contact or STC."

"Oh great, another acronym," I complained, while writing 'S-T-C' in my notebook. "Just what the world needs. What's wrong with 'ADC' anyway?"

"Call them what you want," he said. "I happen to think that names should be both clear and descriptive. After-death communications or encounters could just as well refer to interactions *between* souls within heaven. And both terms could cover intentional contacts initiated through mediums."

"Okay, then. I'll accept one more acronym for the sake of clarity. When Jane Q. Public is sitting in her kitchen and suddenly hears the voice of her deceased daughter calling from the toaster, we'll chalk it up to another case of STC.

"Do these contacts supply strong evidence for Survival?"

"For the most part, the stories are just the sort of anecdotes that scientists blithely ignore and skeptics gleefully spotlight because they are rarely corroborated and are often subject to alternative ex-

---

[42] Archangel, Diane, *Afterlife Encounters: Ordinary People, Extraordinary Experiences*, Hampton Roads Publishing, 2005.

planations such as coincidence and hallucination. But not all anecdotes are created equal. A few are worthy of being added to the Survival Files.

"Now, don't get me wrong," he cautioned, "I doubt neither the accuracy nor the sincerity of the percipients in other cases, especially since so many of them were hard-nosed skeptics prior to their experience. Furthermore, as a firm believer in an afterlife, I have no problem assuming that most of the events related to Arcangel and the Guggenheims did involve communications with the deceased. Nevertheless, if I were attempting to convince a non-believer, I wouldn't find more than a half dozen of the tales worth relating."

"What do the tales-worth-telling have in common? Are the visiting spirits especially solid and life-like?"

"No. Opacity is irrelevant," he replied. "Although many people falsely assume that there is a direct correlation between realism and reality."

I gave him a questioning tilt of my head.

"Over and over again, in book after book, people adamantly deny that their experience was a hallucination because it was 'too real.' Apparently, most folks don't know the meaning of the term. A 'hallucination' is, by definition, an experience that seems absolutely real — but isn't. If the experience seems unreal, then it isn't a hallucination, it's a dream or a fantasy or a bad trip.

"It isn't uncommon for the human brain to be tricked into believing false data. So, when evaluating the strength of evidence, one should ignore all statements of personal belief in 'how real' the event seemed.

"The more evidential stories in *Hello From Heaven*, *Afterlife Encounters*, and similar compilations of testimony, are those wherein the manifesting soul conveys information of some sort that is not available to the percipient via normal channels. In one case related by the Guggenheims, for instance, a friend, whom a woman had last known to be entering the priesthood, appeared to her, a decade later, inexplicably dressed in a Navy uniform. She only found out afterwards that he had become a Navy chaplain and had been killed on the day she saw his spirit.[43]

"In another case, a young woman, who thought her father was in excellent health, had a vision of him in spirit and heard him laugh and claim that now he wouldn't have to pay for the new furniture. Then the phone rang and she was told that her father had died. Later on, she found out that her mother had bought an extravagant

---

[43] Guggenheim, p. 244.

amount of new furniture just before her father's unexpected heart attack."[44]

"These are good evidence for paranormal phenomena of one sort or another," I pointed out, "but I don't see them as unequivocal support for the survival of a conscious personality. I mean, there were bound to be lots of people who knew the woman's old friend during the time he was a Navy chaplain. She could have been reading their minds, couldn't she? Likewise, the daughter could have been reading her mother's mind about both the furniture and her father's death."

"I reckon. Although you might recall a discussion we had earlier about the significance of telepathy. But," he continued, "there are several cases the Guggenheims cite in which deceased loved ones appear and give directions to find money, stocks, insurance policies, and the like that the mourners did not know existed."

"That sounds familiar," I said.

"It should. The literature of the paranormal contains many such cases. One of my favorites was reported back in 1891."[45] He carefully placed his tea cup and saucer on the glass atop the Sheraton

[44] *Ibid*, p. 246.

[45] Myers, F.W.H., *Human Personality and Its Survival of Bodily Death*, 1961 edition, p. 228.

console table between us and sat back in a contented manner. I prepared myself for a nice long story.

The Farmer's Daughter

"It was on February the 2nd of that year ..."

"Tell me," I interjected, "do you think that those who die on Groundhog Day can see their shadow when they come out of the tunnel into the light?"

Amazingly, he didn't even crack a smile at my brilliant wit. "On the second day of February, 1891," he repeated and then continued, "Michael Conley, a farmer from Ionia, Iowa, suffered the indignity of crossing over while sitting in an outhouse in the town of Dubuque, some 110 miles from his home. His body was taken to the local coroner's office and prepared for shipment to his family. In the process, his soiled and rather smelly clothing was removed and thrown on the ground out back of the morgue.

"When Conley's son brought the coffin home, one of his sisters (that is, a daughter of the deceased) fainted and could not be revived for several hours. When she finally awoke, she reported that the spirit of her father had appeared to her and told her that he had sewn a considerable amount of money inside his gray shirt. He had used, she said, a piece of red fabric from an old dress of hers.

"Well, the family was most dubious, but on the advice of their doctor, they tried to placate the nearly hysterical daughter by calling the morgue and asking if the farmer's clothing was still in their possession. On being located in the rubble, the seeming pile of rags was bundled up and given to the son when he arrived to fetch them. As you surely have guessed by now, a rather large roll of bills was soon discovered, wrapped in a red cloth and sewn to the inside of Conley's discarded shirt."

"Well, that's certainly one of your more earthy stories," I said. "Can we trust anything that comes from that period in mid-America? I understand that editors of the time were wont to make up tall tales in the hope of boosting the circulation of their newspapers."

"I cannot deny that possibility," he replied, "although there are a couple of reasons to think this story more credible. First of all, the newspaper involved had already carried the story of Conley's death a week before it reported the incident of the money being found in the shirt. Secondly, F.W.H. Myers, one of the most respected and hard-headed investigators of psychic claims, wrote that the case seemed to have been `carefully and promptly investigated.' "

"Well then," I continued playing devil's advocate, "perhaps the daughter had sewn the money into the shirt for her father. After all, the pocket was made from her dress. Perhaps she and her dad were hatching some nefarious plot and, when she realized the money was gone, she faked a faint until she could invent a story that would retrieve the shirt."

"That's good skeptical analysis, but it seems that the investigators considered this possibility, for they made special note of the fact that the stitches on the inner pocket 'were large and irregular, and looked to be those of a man.' Furthermore, the woman fainted as soon as she saw her father's coffin. (Her brother, wanting to be certain of the corpse's identity before alarming the rest of the family, had not told her why he was traveling to Dubuque.) At the time she asked about the clothing, she had not seen how her father's body was dressed, so she wouldn't have known that his gray shirt had been removed."

"Okay. I accept it, but I wouldn't call it one of the strongest cases."

"I didn't say the story was the most evidential," he avowed, picking up his teacup once more, "I merely said it was one of my favorites."

Grave Mistakes

After a moment quietly contemplating the universe and savoring his tea, the old man got back to the subject at hand. "As for my favorite cases in the more current literature, I am particularly impressed by the story of Cody in *Hello From Heaven*. Cody was a boy who passed on at the age of two and came back to tell his mother that his tombstone had been put on the wrong grave and that his name was 'backwards.'[46] His mother, who had not been to the cemetery since the monument was supposedly installed, checked and discovered that, indeed, the stone had been mistakenly placed on the grave of a little girl who had died 2 weeks prior to her son."

"I can see why you like that one. Unless the installers intentionally screwed up, the improper placement was a fact known to no living person."

"Not only that," he elaborated, "but it was information about a situation that only existed after the death of the communicator. You know, so many of the cases which entail 'knowledge unknown to anyone living' involve info that *was* known to someone at one time. Those folks who are willing to swallow any explanation other than Survival —

---

[46] Guggenheim, p. 285.

no matter how unlikely, or preposterous — might claim that the knowledge somehow lingered in the atmosphere (or the Akashic Records) until sensed by the percipient. The information that Cody communicated to his mother, on the other hand, was never known to anyone at any time until Cody's discarnate mind observed a situation and deduced a conclusion. Thus, it demonstrates the ability of a discarnate soul, not only to communicate with us, but to be aware of events on this plane, to rationally analyze those events, and to emotionally react to them."

"Yes," I agreed, "that is extremely evidential. Why do you speak of Cody reacting emotionally? Did he seem upset when he appeared to his mother?"

"The book doesn't say, but the fact that he made the effort necessary to communicate suggests a high level of concern. Although he likely cared more about soothing his mother's grief than about the placement of a stone."

"Was the boy's name actually backwards?"

"It was not spelled backwards, but it was facing backwards. Once his mother located it, she noticed that the stone was oriented opposite from all the others in the cemetery."

"So," I wondered, "a 2-year-old was able to read well enough to know which way the letters on the stones were oriented?"

"The boy's body may have been young, but I think his soul must have been a bit older — perhaps a few millennia or so."

"You know, there's something very familiar about those switched tombstones."

"Perhaps you are remembering the tale of the elderly man who died and was buried in West Sussex, England, but whose ghost kept haunting the dreams of his daughter, complaining that his fine tombstone had been erected on another man's grave. When asked, the sexton insisted that such a mistake was impossible because his own brother had died just after the old man and was buried in the very next plot. This assurance failed to placate the spirit and, finally, to save the daughter's sanity, an exhumation order was obtained and the markers were, indeed, found to be on the wrong graves. Once the mistake was corrected, the daughter was no longer haunted.

"It makes for an entertaining story, but it comes to us second-hand[47] and lacks corroboration, so it has no value as evidence."

"As I recall, Arcangel's book also contains a case centering around a grave marker."

"Yes, and an especially interesting case it is.[48] A man has a lucid dream in which a friend who died one year previously is standing beside a headstone. 'Call my mother,' the friend says, 'and tell her I love my headstone.' When the man awakes, he draws a picture of the stone and then calls his friend's mother. She tells him that the stone was just set the day before. He immediately drives to the cemetery and discovers that his sketch has captured the actual stone in every detail."

"Well, this could be a case of astral travel," I pointed out, "although the precise timing of his vision argues in favor of spirit involvement. I'm not sure why the case is of such special interest, though."

"The specialness lies in the fact that the man's dream was his second contact with his friend's spirit. In the first, which occurred six months earli-

---

[47] "Correspondence Concerning Evidence for Survival," *Journal of the Society for Psychical Research*, Vol. 24, 1928, p. 336.

[48] Arcangel, pp. 93-95.

er, he could only see blackness as he heard his buddy saying that he was in hell. (Apparently this was due to a crime he had committed.) About two years after the headstone incident, the man had a third dream in which he asks his buddy how he managed to escape from hell. 'I got out,' the friend replied, 'the moment I forgave myself!' "

I nodded my support of that concept, which was in line with the picture of the afterlife we had examined previously. "Do any more of Arcangel's cases stand out?"

He thought for a moment and said: "Do you recall the case of Uncle Jerry's watch?"

"I certainly do. It involved the medium Leonora Piper and the spirit of a man who told of various things he and his brothers did as youths in England. He was Sir Oliver Lodge's uncle and his spirit responded to a gold watch that had belonged to him."

"A most accurate summary," he said. "Now we shall segue from the case of Uncle Jerry's watch to the case of Granddaughter Jerri's watch.[49]

---

[49] Arcangel, pp. 8-9. The author admits to altering some of the names to protect the privacy of the percipients, so this might not be such a coincidence after all.

Grandma's Gift

"This tale is related by a young woman whose best friend, Jerri, excitedly showed her a watch she had received as a Christmas present from her grandmother. It seems that the grandmother had purchased the watch, wrapped it, and hidden it away — and then departed for heaven just before the holidays. Jerri found the watch only because she had an STC in which her grandma gave her very specific directions: 'Look in the bottom of my big sewing box in the back of the closet in the spare bedroom. ... it's wrapped in a red and green box.' Both Jerri's mom and grandpa dismissed the encounter as merely a dream. They were most amazed when the watch was found just as indicated."

"I like your favorite stories," I said. "While we're on the subject of STCs, do you have a least-favorite case?"

Jumping to Confusion

"Well, there are certainly many cases reported that add nothing to the body of evidence for Survival. That doesn't mean that they aren't sincere, however, and they are often entertaining. The only gripe I have about some instances of spirit contact — whether via STCs, NDEs, mediums, or whatever — is the way in which the messages can be distorted by the percipients to endorse their own particular ideology."

"You mean how some people jump to the conclusion that the loving being of light they perceive is actually Moses or Mohammed or whoever is the major figure in their religion?"

"Yes, even though the entity never actually makes such a claim.

"Perhaps the most extreme example I've ever read of this didn't even involve a loving light. It is the case of a mail carrier named Glen.[50] Early one morning, according to his account, Glen had a vision in which his son and his ex-wife appeared looking healthy and happy. Glen, who up 'til that moment had been an atheist, realized that his son was in heaven and, he says: 'All of sudden, I believed! I knew that God, Jesus, the Holy Ghost, the saints, and everything that I had been taught was true!'

"Now, neither Glen's son nor his ex-wife mentioned anything about God or Jesus, let alone 'the saints.' But, once Glen's mind accepted the evidence for an afterlife it blindly jumped to the conclusion that all the associated religious concepts it had been taught in Sunday school must also be

---

[50] Guggenheim, p. 372-3.

correct. This sort of overreaction is all too typical of new converts. Perhaps this is another reason that more people don't experience STCs."

"How so?" I asked.

"The spirits might be afraid that their appearance will reinforce latent, and erroneous, religious beliefs, thus contributing to the already plethoric zealotry and divisiveness in this world."

I decided to shift focus slightly. "Aside from the matter of evidence, are STCs useful in learning about heaven?"

"Not very. Many, if not most, communications are from souls who are still earthbound. And even if they have gone on, apparently it takes a while for souls, even old souls, to become adjusted to their new surroundings and remember who they really are. Only then are they able to accurately perceive the higher realms. So, the recently deceased can't provide us much information about the conditions in heaven, and they almost never mention reincarnation. Nevertheless, what they do describe fits well with the picture of heaven we have built up from other sources.

"One intriguing point of agreement, by the way, is not with the destination but with the means of entrance and egress. Several of the folks interviewed by the Guggenheims told of visions in which they traveled through a tunnel to reach heaven and to return to this plane."[51]

"Wow! That further weakens the überskeptic's argument that all those tunnels reported in near-death experiences are merely an effect of brain cells expiring ."

"Well, that argument was dead anyway," he said. "But I suppose these tunnel experiences of healthy folks are additional nails in its coffin."

Resisting Review

"These souls you speak of that are earthbound, why do you suppose there are so many of them?" I asked. "Why would so many spirits not be attracted to a warm and loving light? Why would they want to avoid heaven?"

"I'm sure there are quite a few who just haven't gotten around to focusing on that light because they are so concerned with monitoring, and possibly trying to influence, events in the physical world. As for the others, well, it may not be that spirits are afraid of going to heaven; it could be that what they truly dread is the entrance exam."

"The entrance exam?"

---

[51] Guggenheim, pp. 174-181. Also, see Botkin and Hogan's *Induced After-Death Communication*, pp. 149-152.

"Over and over, both spirit contacts and NDErs report that each soul undergoes a life review as part of the process of entering heaven. During this review, the souls experience the effect they have had on other people. According to many reports, this experience is from the other person's point of view. It is not actually an 'exam,' but it can be a dreadful experience. Imagine that you were a bit of a bully in your youth and liked to tease, beat-up, and otherwise terrorize those smaller and weaker than you. After you've met your demise — and once you accept the fact that you are still a conscious being — you realize that in order to move on, you must go through a process in which you will feel all the horror and hurt that you inflicted upon others. Plus, you will feel it much more strongly than your victims did, because disembodied spirits are far more sensitive to all emotions than embodied ones are."

"Yes, we touched on that in our previous conversations."

"Well, it bears emphasizing. If *you* were such a bully (and the world has certainly had its share of them) how anxious would *you* be to cross that threshold?"

"The world has had its share of much worse than that," I pointed out. "Child molesters, rapists, axe murderers, and the like must be especially fearful of experiencing the pain they caused."

"And then there are those who face even tougher life reviews," he said.

"Even tougher than child molesters and serial killers?"

"Imagine what awaits those who, for their own advancement or to promote their own causes, have brought war upon the world. Even the hardiest would tremble at the thought of having to experience all the pain of all the soldiers dead or mutilated in battle, not to mention the anguish of their widows and loved ones."

"Ouch! And some say there is no such thing as punishment."

"Don't think of the life review as punishment," he remonstrated. "Remember that we are all tiny parts of God and God is not a masochist. He has no interest in punishing Himself in any form or for any reason.

"Think of it more as making the most of the experience. The life review brings the cause and the effect together into an easily comprehended whole. The pain and the perpetrator become one. The agony is merged with the ecstasy. Thus, the experience is clarified and the gestalt is closed."

"But if all these souls avoid the life review by hanging around the physical plane, there must be an awful lot of unfinished business."

"There is — for the moment — but our moments are very brief in the celestial time frame. Sooner or later, everybody moves on. At least, that is what the spirits assert and what we all hope."

Alfred Russel Wallace

British naturalist and explorer, co-originator with Charles Darwin of the natural selection theory of evolution, and known to many as the "Grand Old Man of Science." Wallace was awarded honorary doctorates by both the University of Dublin and by Oxford University, and important medals from the Royal Society, the Société de Geographie, the Royal Geographical Society, and the Linnaean Society. Also, he received the Order of Merit from the British Crown. The fact that he never had to protect a tenured position at a major university may explain his willingness to challenge establishment views.

In His Own Words:

"Up to the time when I first became acquainted with the facts of Spiritualism, I was a confirmed philosophical sceptic, rejoicing in the works of Voltaire, Strauss, and Carl Vogt, and an ardent admirer (as I am still) of Herbert Spencer. I was so thorough and confirmed a materialist that I could not at that time find a place in my mind for the conception of spiritual existence, or for any other agencies in the universe than matter and force.

"Facts, however, are stubborn things. My curiosity was at first excited by some slight but inexplicable phenomena occurring in a friend's family, and my desire for knowledge and love of truth forced me to continue the inquiry. The facts became more and more assured, more and more varied, more and more removed from anything that modern science taught or modern philosophy speculated on. The facts beat me. They compelled me to accept them as facts long before I could accept the spiritual explanation of them; there was at that time no place in my fabric of thought into which it could be fitted. By slow degrees a place was made; but it was made, not by any preconceived or theoretical opinions, but by the continuous action of fact after fact, which could not be got rid of in any other way."[52]

---

[52] Wallace, Alfred Russel, *Miracles and Modern Spiritualism*, George Redway, 1896, pp. vi-vii.

Invited Spirit Conversations

I dismiss the whole question of fraud from the phenomena so emphatically that I should not waste any time on the skeptic who still insists on that point of view. He is either too ignorant or too indolent for us any longer to attach any value to his convictions. … Our business is not with him, but with honest people.

— Professor James H. Hyslop[53]

The following three cases taken from the Survival Top 40 all involve information intentionally sought from a specific spirit and delivered via a medium who had no normal access to that information.

Friends and Strangers
[Case ID# 48, ESS Score = 275, Current Rank 8th]

George Pellew was trained as a lawyer and was the author of at least six books, including a well-known biography of the first Chief Justice of the United States,

---

[53] *Proceedings of the American Society for Psychical Research,*
   1925, p. 2.

John Jay. Pellew was a member of the Society for Psychical Research but, in common with many SPR members, he did *not* believe that the human personality survived the demise of its physical body. He and Richard Hodgson, one of the chief researchers for the SPR, were closely acquainted and had enjoyed several lengthy discussions on metaphysical matters. In February, 1892, at the age of 32, Pellew was killed in an accident in New York City.

On March 22, a little over a month after Pellew's death, Hodgson began to arrange sittings for Pellew's friends with the trance-medium Leonora Piper – sittings in which Pellew made himself known. For these, and in all published materials, Pellew was referred to by the pseudonym "George Pelham" or, simply "G.P." Apparently influenced by the Victorian sense of propriety, a great deal of care was taken not to identify people or reveal any personal matters that were discussed. The result was that a great deal – probably the bulk – of evidence developed in the Pellew sessions was never made public. Even so, a significant amount was published, as the spirit of George Pellew actively participated in virtually all of Piper's sessions for more than five years. The majority of Pellew's communications were achieved via automatic writing.

Throughout his tenure, over 150 persons participated in sessions with Piper, of whom about 30 were friends or acquaintances of Pellew. Remarkably, he seemed always to recognize with "the appropriate emotional and intellectual relations" those he knew in the past, and to treat as strangers those whom he had never met.

There were actually two exceptions to Pellew's "always" recognizing only those whom he knew. One occurred on January 7, 1897. The sitter, a young woman given the name "Miss Warner," had attended a session the day before and mentioned that she had known Pellew, yet he had not acknowledged her. During this second session, he asked her who she was. Hodgson spoke up and told Pellew that the woman's mother was a friend of his. The conversation proceeded:

[G.P.] I do not think I ever knew you very well.

[Warner] Very little. You used to come and see my mother.

I heard of you, I suppose.

I saw you several times. You used to come with Mr. Rogers.

Yes, I remembered about Mr. Rogers when I saw you before.

Yes, you spoke of him.

Yes, but I cannot seem to place you. I long to place all of my friends, and could do so before I had been gone so long. You see I am farther away. ... I do not recall your face. You must have changed.

At this point Hodgson asked, "Do you remember Mrs. Warner?" Immediately Piper's writing hand showed excitement.

> Of course, oh, very well. For pity sake. Are you her little daughter?

Yes.

> By Jove, how you have grown. I thought so much of your mother, a charming woman.

She always enjoyed seeing you, I know.

> Our tastes were similar.

About writing?

> Do you know Marte at all?

I've met him once or twice.

> Your mother knows. Ask her if she remembers the book I gave her to read.

I will.

> And ask her if she still remembers me and the long talks we used to have at the home evenings.

I know she does.

> I wish I could have known you better, it would have been so nice to have recalled the past.

I was a little girl.

Hodgson asks his readers to remember that "these sittings were held five years after the death of G. P., and that G. P. had not seen Miss Warner for at least three or four years before his death, that she was only a little girl when he had last seen her, that she had not been, so to say, a special friend of his, and that she had, indeed, changed very much in the intervening eight or nine years. This non-recognition, then, by G. P. is a perfectly natural circumstance."

The second (apparent) exception to Pellew's perfect memory also adds to the strength of the evidence, but in the opposite way. It occurred when a man known as "Mr. Savage" was a sitter. Hodgson believed that Pellew was meeting Savage for the first time, a belief in which Savage concurred. Nevertheless Pellew seemed familiar with the man. Hodgson asked, "Do you know this gentleman, M. J. Savage?" Pellew replied, "Yes. I do. How are you, sir? Speak to me. This is too delightful. I am so pleased to see your face again." Hodgson persisted, "You remember meeting him in the body?" "Oh yes, well. I do, well."

Hodgson reports that he was "surprised at the amount of feeling indicated both by the words written and the excitement of the hand." Later, however, Hodgson recalled that George Pellew had, while living, attended one sitting with Piper and that Savage was an SPR Committee Officer who was present officially at the sitting. At that time, Pellew was not introduced under his real name, and it was noted in the report of the sitting that he was unknown to Savage. Clearly, though, Pellew's spirit recalled with some excitement meeting Savage some six years previously when he was in the position of the sitter, instead of his current position as communicator.

The Pellew sessions thus offer excellent evidence that Piper's success was not due to reading the minds of the living. All the strangers attending a session certainly held their own names clearly in their conscious minds yet, when Pellew was acting as control, he never greeted them by name. Even when the sitter held a memory of meeting Pellew, he could not derive her name because he did not recognize her physically as a past acquaintance. But he did greet all those he knew, even one who had forgotten he knew him. It is this last point — the insistence by the spirit of a truth counter to the thoughts of both the sitter and the witness — upon which hinges the uncommonly high rating for the case.

All this indicates a human personality acting precisely as would be expected of one who had survived death. Or, as Hodgson put it, "This recognition of friends appears to me to be of great importance evidentially, not only because it indicates some supernormal knowledge, but because, when all the circumstances are taken into consideration, they seem to point, in G. P.'s case, to an independent intelligence drawing upon its own recollections."

A Mysterious Death
[Case ID# 39, ESS Score = 277, Current Rank 7th]

Edgar Vandy was a brilliant young engineer and inventor who lived in London with his family (mother, sister, and two brothers). At the time of his death, in 1933, Edgar[54] was involved with several engineering projects involving telephony, radio, and other electro-mechanical devices. His largest and most promising project was known as the Lectroline Drawing Machine, a machine that could precisely create lines and lettering on plates suitable for use on printing presses. The Lectroline could enable one person to do the work of several craftsmen. A lot of time and family money had been expended in the creation of this machine, and the details of the prototype's operation were a closely guarded secret.

On August 6, 1933, Edgar went for a ride in the country with a friend, referred to only as Mr. Jameson[55] or "N.J." and Jameson's sister. They ended up at an estate in Sussex owned by the sister's employer, who was not there at the time. It being a particularly hot and very sunny day, the trio decided to go for a swim in a pool on the estate grounds. The pool was lined with concrete and had a diving board, but the bottom

---

[54] First names are used here to distinguish among Edgar and his brothers.

[55] A pseudonym.

was coated with slime and sediment that, when stirred up, made the water so cloudy that one could see no more than a few inches beneath the surface.

Such a condition of dense turbidity was what confronted Edgar's would-be rescuers when they arrived in response to Jameson's summons. Although only seven feet down, the body could not be seen, even when the pool was half-drained.

At the inquest, Jameson testified that he and Edgar had gone behind heavy shrubbery some ways from the pool to change into swim wear. Edgar had not brought a swimsuit so Jameson's sister loaned him one. Edgar changed quicker and went ahead. When Jameson arrived he saw Edgar floating face down in the water. Jumping in immediately, Jameson tried to save him, but he slipped from his grasp and sank. Jameson then retreated from the pool and went to find help, which did not arrive until an hour later.

The doctor who was present when Edgar's body was pulled from the murky water, noted that there were slight abrasions beneath the chin and the tongue had been bitten through. Some scrapes were also found on the body's left side and right shoulder. Also, there was less fluid in the lungs than usual in drowning victims. These facts led to the theory that the young man had struck his jaw while diving into the pool and been knocked unconscious. The coroner accepted all of this testimony and returned a verdict of "Death by Drowning by Misadventure."

Edgar's two brothers, Harold and George Vandy, were not satisfied with this verdict. From a contemporary standpoint, in a world full of forensic TV dramas, it is easy to sympathize with their doubts. Actually, we can only marvel at their restraint in not raising specific questions. How, for instance, did the pool water get so stirred up that it was still impenetrable an hour after Jameson climbed out? Or, was the water always so turbid? If so, is it conceivable that a highly intelligent man would have dived into it without any idea what lay beneath? (Edgar, by the way, was a poor swimmer and was never known to dive into anything.)

Perhaps most out of the ordinary is that a man unfamiliar with a place would "go ahead," leaving his friend to finish changing alone. Also difficult to believe is that Jameson could not manage to drag Edgar, who was not a large fellow, to safety in such a small and fairly shallow pool with no currents or other endangering conditions. And what would possess someone to think that they could find help in less time than it would take for a man to drown?

Then there is the matter of the sister who clearly instigated the visit to her boss' home, encouraged Edgar to enter the pool by providing him with a swim suit from who-knows-where, and then seems to have disappeared forever. She did not appear to help her brother rescue Edgar; she did not appear at the inquest, and couldn't be traced later. The fact that she worked for a very wealthy (and thus influential) man who likely didn't appreciate any bad publicity sullying his estate is more than cause for suspicion that the inquest was not entirely above board.

The Vandy brothers, however, voiced no such misgivings, at least not publicly. Their only stated goal was to clear up "some doubts" regarding the cause of Edgar's death. Although they did not at first believe in an afterlife, they hoped that a trance medium might be able to tap into some mind or another and uncover the truth via ESP.

George had once heard the Reverend Drayton Thomas lecture on proxy sittings whereby a person who knows little or nothing of a case "sits in" for a more involved person. (This should rule out the medium pulling key information from, or otherwise being influenced by, the mind of the sitter.) So George wrote to the Rev. Thomas asking him to proxy sit with the medium Gladys Osborne Leonard. This sitting was granted but it could not be scheduled for several weeks, and the brothers made other arrangements in the interim. Altogether, over a period of a year, nearly a dozen separate sessions were held with at least four mediums. (An additional sitting was held some 23 years later with yet another medium.)[56]

In the archives of psychic research one would be hard pressed to find any other case of a private citizen's death being so thoroughly and repetitively investigated. The inordinate number of mediums and sittings makes for a complex case that can be difficult to grasp in its entirety. For our purposes, we'll consider all the evidence as coming from one "super séance" and present only key statements therefrom. Nevertheless, it is important to note that the repetition of many descriptions and ideas among the various mediums makes an excellent counter to those who claim that a medium's correct statements are simply lucky guesses. Those who strongly resist the idea of a spirit world may be able to credit one correct statement to fortune, but when three or more mediums all come up with the same information, only the most desperate überskeptic will dare claim luck or coincidence.

Of course, some would claim collusion. This is why the Vandy brothers went to such lengths to conceal their identities. Each initial appointment was made under a false name by mail from a different address. They never attended sessions together and they did not

---

[56] In order of consultation, the mediums were: Miss Frances Campbell, Mrs. Gladys Osbourne Leonard, Mrs. Mason, Miss Naomi Bacon, and Mrs. Bertha Harris.

look at all alike. There was no normal way in which any medium could have known the identity of either Harold or George. They even hired different note takers to accompany them to each new medium. Furthermore, during the sessions they were most reticent to answer the medium's requests for confirmation of her statements.

Making the extent of the case even more exceptional is the underlying skepticism of the brothers. Although deeply desirous of information, they persisted in assuming that recognized facts were gleaned via telepathy from the minds of the living and unrecognized statements were false until proven true. Ultimately, though, they seemed to accept that some part of their brother Edgar had survived the murky water.

Each medium consulted seemed to make contact with the spirit of Edgar Vandy. Out of all the hundreds of statements made by the various mediums, a few of those demonstrating paranormal knowledge appear below. Each statement by a medium (or her control, or a contact) is followed by the relevant facts.

Statement: (As the medium points to her front teeth) He is showing me a little gap in his mouth as if a tooth were missing. Now he shows me an old scar and says 'That's my identification mark!' [Sitter: "Where is the scar?"] On his face.

Facts: The cutting edge of one of Edgar's upper teeth had broken off, leaving a small gap between that and the corresponding lower tooth. He also had a large scar on the right side of his forehead, obtained by being thrown from a trap as a child. George had heard him make the remark, "This scar will always identify me."

Statement: Now he is showing me a cigarette case, and that's funny, because he did not smoke. [Sitter: "I don't think he had a cigarette case."] He tells me where to find it — in his room — it seems to be at the end of a passage — there's a chest of drawers near the window. In one of the drawers you will find his things carefully folded up. I think you will find it there. [Sitter: "He didn't have a cigarette case."] Put it down and check it up.

Facts: True, Edgar did not smoke.[57] The evening after the sitting Harold and George looked in the chest of drawers (which was near a window) and found Edgar's underwear carefully folded as described. They did not find a cigarette case, but in a corner at the bottom there was a new aluminum soap box. This, when held in the hand as shown by the medium, looked exactly like a metal cigarette case.

Statement: He had a watch. [Sitter: "No."] He had a watch that wouldn't go.

Facts: "I found afterwards that he had a wrist watch."
— George Vandy

---

[57] In that era, the odds were that the young man *did* smoke cigarettes.

Statement: This young man had a lot of papers that he kept in a kind of flat book form... there was quite a pile of them. But there was one of them that had both writing and drawings in it that he had done ... some of them had brown, and some it looks almost like black covers on them.

Facts: These notebooks were unknown to the brothers until George found them while clearing out a storeroom more than 30 years later. All had black stiff covers except one, which had brown.

Statement: Now he's showing me a tennis racquet. He is holding it up like this (holding her two hands diagonally), and that's strange, because he didn't play tennis. He doesn't look like a fellow who would play tennis. [Sitter: "I don't understand the racquet. He didn't play tennis."] Make a note of it and check it up.

Facts: Edgar did not play tennis or possess a racquet. When the incident was mentioned to their sister, she related that, a few weeks previously, she had a spare exposure on a spool of film and she used it to take a photograph of Edgar in the garden. It was a bright sunny day and he was dressed in tennis shirt, trousers, and shoes. To complete the picture, his sister fetched her racquet and asked him to pose with it. He joked about it and said the picture would delude people into thinking he was a player.

Statement: Your other brother makes short journeys in his work. I get the letter "H". He is wearing something belonging to your brother who has passed over. [Sitter: "I don't think that is right. What is it?"] I think it is an article of clothing. [Sitter: "I'm sure that's not right."] He's persistent about it. Check it up.

Facts: "One morning after Edgar's death, Harold took one of Edgar's hats by mistake. He did not return it but left it at the office with no intention of wearing it. On the day of this sitting his own hat was uncomfortable, so in the afternoon, almost involuntarily, he took Edgar's hat off the peg in his office and wore it. He was wearing it at the time the sitting took place. I knew nothing of this until I discussed the incident with Harold after the sitting." — George Vandy

Statement: Do you know why he was interested in wireless [radio]? He seems very interested in it. In fact he keeps using wireless terms; he calls this a transmission. He is showing me the letters B.B.C.

Facts: Edgar was keenly interested in wireless and had an expert knowledge of the subject. In the early days of the industry he ran a small manufacturing business. He and George were founding shareholders in the original British Broadcasting Company.

Statement: This is a fairly big thing he is trying to show me, and has a wooden board, and he presses something, and I get something rolling forward and then a click, click, click, that is the thing he is trying to tell me about. Do you know he is not trying to write up something, but he is showing me a lot of letters : A, B, C, D, etc., and he shuffles them about a bit with his hands, and then he shows me a funny thing just like a thin line, and then an arm comes up and projects about half-a-dozen letters.

Facts: The Lectroline was about 6-feet square with a large wooden drawing board. It was started by pushing a button and controlled with rolls of paper tape. It made loud clicking sounds as it worked. Few, if any, other machines of the time would fit the description given.

Statement: Would lithography or something of that work come into it? He says lithography or something to do with printing and I think he was clever in something he was helping to do. There were more machines, but he did a particular thing, and I do not know whether photography comes into it as well, but he is trying to show me plates or something. It seems to be very fine work, but in the actual room he is in I do not get many machines, but one special machine. In other parts of the building there are more, but he had a special thing.

Facts: The primary output of the machine was lithographic plates. "The last attachment Edgar made for the Lectroline was a device for ruling very fine lines. In order to test how fine and close together he could draw the lines he used an old photographic negative and replaced the pen by a razor edge he specially made. In an adjoining room of the premises are seven copper-plate printing presses and an engraving machine." — Harold Vandy

Statement: May I ask a question? Have I given his initials all right? [Sitter did not respond.] There is a 'D' in it - Ed. - Ed. - Ed - gar or Ed - ward. - Edgar.

Facts: Which is, of course, correct.

An important counter to the idea that all was done by reading the minds of the living should be noted here. One brother, Harold, was in the real estate business and totally ignorant of the operations of Edgar's inventions; the second brother, George, was an engineer who was generally familiar with the machines; Edgar's assistant, John Burke, also had one sitting with one of the same mediums. Burke was an engineer who had worked on the equipment from the start. If the mediums were reading minds to gain their information, one would reasonably expect the more technical information to result from sittings with the more technically oriented and knowledgeable sitters. Exactly the opposite was the case. The séances with Harold produced the most attempts to describe machinery. The session with Burke, who was well versed in every aspect of the equipment, produced nothing technical whatsoever.

As for *how* Edgar died, many intriguing comments were passed along by the mediums. Some examples are:

- *He passed out through water, and yet it seems it need not have happened. I do not think it was a swimming bath. I am in a private kind of pool, and I am getting diving and things like that. Yes, I am out-of-doors, I am not enclosed — it is like a private swimming pool.*

- *He did not commit suicide, and he says he was not foolish, it was not his fault. He was after a definite object. There was somebody else. There was another person? His death was quite sudden.*

- *Your brother is talking a little as if he were afraid. That is curious, he is telling me that there is a woman who can tell you more about him (he is pointing to himself). This will puzzle you very much, as you cannot in any way connect it up. "I tell you she was frightened and went away," he says. When I ask him to explain more, he just nods. "That is right, it was to do with my passing over, but no one knew she was there."*

- *It is something about having to get his clothes. He had taken some of his clothing off. He gives me exactly the condition he was in, he was ill for only two or three minutes before he passed out, dazed, I get a quick drop. Even in the time he took to fall, the whole mind seemed to be upon his clothes. Your brother was very shy by nature.*

- *It was not his fault, he says "It was not my fault." There was a funny feeling in his head, a woolly head, muddled, I feel; he gives me that feeling purposely after what you said — it was something he felt before, while, and even now, when he thinks of his passing.*

- *He certainly had a blow, and I am getting as though he were semi-conscious when he was in the water. From what I see of the conditions it is as though it were strange that he was drowned. I feel that he can tell me more than he will tell me, but he might implicate someone else. That is what I feel, and he does not want to give it.*

- *It seems to be something which happened under very unusual conditions, as far as he is trying to show me. He seems to be very unwilling to assist me just now.*

- *Is it right that you cannot get accurate information as to what happened, and that they did not tell you, and there is something being hushed up, because he is saying "I do not think you will be able to prove it on earth. It is something which was done and I do not know whether you will really get the truth about it."*

- *If this other person who was with him had not been cowardly, it would not have happened. This other man knows about it and will not say. I do not know if he was frightened and got out of the way and left him, because he is asking me to tell you that.*

- *I am not sure if someone was diving at the time. There was a diving board and whether someone knocked him or not I do not know, because he remembers going under and feeling a distinct blow on the head. He could not come up, as he apparently lost consciousness under water. This water should have been transparent, and it is very extraordinary nobody saw that, but he distinctly said*

there was another man there at the same time who
should have known he was hurt.

And so, the cause of Edgar Vandy's physical demise seems destined to remain mysterious. One of the
mediums opined: "I do not think he is capable yet to
give the evidence that I wanted him to." But was he
incapable or unwilling? And, if unwilling, who was he
protecting?

New Meaning for "Soul Mate"
[Case ID# 24, ESS Score = 278, Current Rank 4th]

If you've spent any time puttering around chess sites
on the Web, you might have encountered a story about
a game played between two chess masters, only one of
whom was alive at the time! Those telling the tale generally assume that it is bogus or was an April Fool's
joke or they find some other way to disassociate themselves from such an outrageous idea. Their ignorance is
quite understandable, for the full story was only available in the German language until quite recently.

There are two parts to this story: the interview and
the game. The interview contains a great deal of compelling evidence; nevertheless, the game is the more
unusual and therefore interesting aspect, so we'll cover
it first.

The Game

When an acquaintance came up with the idea for a chess match played across the great divide, Wolfgang Eisenbeiss, Ph.D., thought that a medium named Robert Rollans might be able to facilitate the competition. Eisenbeiss had worked with Rollans for several years, and felt that the medium had the two necessary qualifications: he was trustworthy and he knew nothing of chess. So, a list of deceased Grandmasters was drawn up and Rollans' spirit control was asked to see if any of them could be located in the spirit realms and persuaded to play a game. While that search went on, Dr. Eisenbeiss sought an earthbound champion willing to compete against a ghost. Perhaps the most amazing thing about this remarkable story is that someone was willing to risk ridicule in the chess world by agreeing to do so. That person was Grandmaster Viktor Korchnoi, who was ranked third in the world at the time.

On the 15th of June, 1985, the challenge was accepted by a spirit claiming to be Géza Maróczy (the name is pronounced GEH-zaw MAHR-ot-see) a Hungarian who had passed from this mortal plane in 1951. Maróczy was also ranked third in the world — during the early 1900s — so the pairing promised to be competitive. [This presentation will refer to this combination of the medium Rollans and the spirit Maróczy/Rollans, or simply M/R.]

Maróczy/Rollans moved first. (It isn't clear how the opener was selected; perhaps it was because ghosts are generally envisioned as being white.) The move was communicated through Rollans via automatic writing, forwarded to Eisenbeiss, who passed it on to Korchnoi. When Korchnoi determined his response, he told Eisenbeiss, who told Rollans. Rollans would then go into his home office, write the move on a piece of paper, and make the move on a small chessboard. (Eisenbeiss, an amateur chess enthusiast, had to give Rollans lessons on chess moves and notation so that the medium would understand enough to move the pieces properly.) The communication of each move typically required about 10 days, but Korchnoi was often out of touch (grandmasters travel a lot) and so the entire match took 7 years and 8 months. Maróczy resigned after 47 moves. Just in time too, as Rollans fell ill toward the end and died only 3 weeks after the match's conclusion.

And how well did the spirit master acquit himself? About as well as one might expect from any champion with Maróczy's training and background. Those readers proficient at chess play and knowledgeable of chess history can judge for themselves by examining the game. The rest of us will have to rely on the testimony of experts. His opponent, Korchnoi, made the following observation after the 27th move: "During the opening phase Maróczy showed weaknesses. His play is old fashioned. But ... I am not sure I will win. He has compensated the faults of the opening by a strong end-game. In the end-game the ability of a player shows up, and my opponent plays very well." Helmut Metz, a well known chess commentator, observed that Korchnoi's opponent "controlled the end-game like the old masters from the first half of the century."[58]

The Moves:

1. e4 e6	13. Bxc6 Bxc6	25. a4 Rxg3	37. Rf5+ Kxg4
2. d4 d5	14. Bg5 d4	26. fxg3 b6	38. h6 b3
3. Nc3 Bb4	15. Bxe7 Kxe7	27. h4 a6	39. h7 Ra8
4. e5 c5	16. Qh4+ Ke8	28. g4 b5	40. cxb3 Rh8
5. a3 Bxc3+	17. Ke2 Bxf3+	29. axb5 axb5	41. Rxf6 Rxh7
6. bxc3 Ne7	18. gxf3 Qxe5+	30. Kd3 Kg6	42. Rg6+ Kf4
7. Dg4 cxd4	19. Qe4 Qxe4+	31. Rf1 Rh8	43. Rf6+ Kg3
8. Qxg7 Rg8	20. fxe4 f6	32. Rh1 Rh7	44. Rf1 Rh2
9. Qxh7 Qc7	21. Rad1 e5	33. Ke2 Ra7	45. Rd1 Kf3
10. Kd1 dxc3	22. Rd3 Kf7	34. Kd3 Ra2	46. Rf1+ Rf2
11. Nf3 Nbc6	23. Rg3 Rg6	35. Rf1 b4	47. Rxf2+ Kxf2
12. Bb5 Bd7	24. Rhg1 Rag8	36. h5+ Kg5	0—1

Playing chess well enough to make a grandmaster unsure of victory is an extremely rare skill. (Chess playing computers that could threaten a grandmaster were not readily available during those years.) Doing

---

[58] See Metz's Website: http://www.rochadekuppenheim.de/meko/meko1a/m12.htm.

so in an "old fashioned" style could only be accomplished by a handful of geniuses ... if by anyone alive today.

Not to accept these events as convincing evidence of Survival would require believing that some unknown player of immense skill and knowledge would be willing to put his reputation at risk by committing fraud over and over again for almost a decade — and without any recognition or compensation!

Mind reading, even on a grand scale, can't explain things either. Picking up impressions may be common, and discerning an occasional message from another's mind is not unheard of, but no one has ever demonstrated an ability to learn a complex skill via telepathy.

But wait ... there's more!

The Interview

At various times over the course of the match, Eisenbeiss asked Maróczy/Rollans to provide information about Maróczy's tournaments and personal life. M/R's initial response was to produce 38 hand-written pages of biographical information. From these pages, Eisenbeiss compiled a list of 39 points (later subdivided by his co-author, Dieter Hassler, into 92 discrete statements) that he thought might be subject to verification.[59] These points were sorted into five categories according to the likelihood of the medium being able to guess or discover the information without spirit help. These categories ranged from the sort of facts that could be gleaned from an ordinary encyclopedia (such as Maróczy's birthplace) through more specialized facts (such as the place Maróczy won in a Monte Carlo tournament in 1903) up to private information shared by few and not known to be written down (such as the level of chess-playing skill displayed by Maróczy's children, and the sort of job that Maróczy took after he finished school[60]).

Eisenbeiss then set about checking the validity of the spirit's statements. First, he asked Korchnoi to verify the statements, but the Grandmaster declined the task, saying that he did not know the facts and it would take too much time and effort to learn them. So, Eisenbeiss put the statements into question format and obtained the services of historian and chess expert László Sebestyén to find the answers. Not told anything of the case and never meeting Rollans or Korchnoi, Mr. Sebestyén worked under the assumption that

---

[59] The *Journal* report of 91 points was corrected in an Erratum sent by Hassler to the author on 23 November 2006.

[60] The spirit had correctly stated that Maróczy was a draftsman for a company that designed municipal water mains.

his research was for an article on Maróczy. Consulting numerous specialized libraries and interviewing Maróczy's two surviving children and a cousin, Sebestyén managed to answer all but seven of the questions. And only three of the historian's answers differed from the statements given by M/R.

Of perhaps greater significance, when only the more difficult questions — 33 pieces of private or hidden information — are considered, 31 were verified and the answers to the remaining two could not be found.[61] None contradicted the spirit's testimony. This gives a confirmed accuracy rate of 94 percent, but if more information could be discovered the rate could well be 100 percent!

Impressive statistics aside, there are a couple of exchanges worthy of special attention. The first revolves around a spelling dispute.

One of the questions involved a match in San Remo, Italy, in which Maróczy made a surprising move that thrilled the spectators and saved a game thought to be lost. For this reason, Eisenbeiss speculated that the game might be recalled by Maróczy, even though it was played almost 60 years earlier against a relatively unknown player from Italy named Romi.

---

[61] These unanswered questions asked the name of Maróczy's first love and the name of a café he liked to frequent in Paris.

As with the chess move that prompted the question, Maróczy/Rollans' response was unexpected — and exceptionally evidential. Maróczy said that he never knew anyone named Romi, but that, as a youth, he did have a friend named Romih (with an "h" at the end) and that this was the man whom he had defeated in San Remo. So, Eisenbeiss asked Sebestyén to determine the correct spelling of the name.

The historian found a German book and a Russian book that mentioned Romi (sans h) but another one by a Hungarian spelled the name Romih, so he felt the matter could not be settled. Eisenbeiss then took up the hunt himself and discovered two more references to Romi, and was about convinced that M/R was incorrect, when he managed to obtain a copy of the official program of the 1930 San Remo Tournament. Therein, the Italian player was mentioned in several places and his name was always spelled Romih. So Maróczy had remembered the name correctly.

Why this spelling discrepancy had occurred was not revealed until Eisenbeiss found a chess expert from Italy who remembered that Max Romih was of Slavonic origin and had emigrated to Italy in 1918. He hadn't dropped the "h" off the end of his name until after the San Remo tournament. Thus, there was no discord in Maróczy claiming to have known this Italian player as a youth in Hungary.

The second of Maróczy/Rollans' statements that deserve special attention concerns a female chess champion named Vera Menchik. On the 4th of August, 1988, an ad in a chess magazine asked readers to answer the question: "Who was the Austrian founder of the Vera Menchik Club?" This club was formed as a lark by players who had lost tournament games to Menchik. As Menchik was known to have been one of Maróczy's pupils, Eisenbeiss put the question to M/R.

On the 8th of August, M/R offered two names as possibly the club's founder; neither was correct. On the 11th, he again expressed uncertainty and mentions a Dr. Becker, but rejects him because Becker had moved to South America. Furthermore, M/R described the club as a "silly joke" that had not captured his attention at the time. On August 18th, the magazine answered its own question: the founder of the Vera Menchik Club was, indeed, Dr. Becker.

During a session on August 21st, the subject was again raised and, despite the fact that the answer was now public knowledge (at least to those who read that particular chess magazine), M/R remained uncertain of the founder's identity. Instead, he changed the subject and told a most revealing story involving the wife and mistress of another world champion. This story is also quite evidential — as are several others in the report — but only the strongest evidence can be examined here.

The difficulty of emulating the play of a Grandmaster from the early 1900s makes any source other than Maróczy's spirit virtually inconceivable. Add to that the knowledge demonstrated of Maróczy's life and his insistence on spelling Romih with a final "h" (despite being contradicted by most available reference works) and one can eliminate the qualifier "virtually." Nor, in light of Maróczy's inability to name the founder of the Vera Menchik Club, is it justifiable to claim the employment of some theoretical and baseless "Super ESP."

It should also be noted that the medium, Rollans, received no compensation for his participation throughout the almost nine years of the match. Neither, by the way, did Korchnoi.[62]

Some have suggested that Rollans could have played as he did by reading the mind of Korchnoi. There are three problems with this idea. First, it does nothing to explain the interview data. Second, it requires that Rollans access Korchnoi's thoughts to an unheard-of degree. And third, if Rollans knew what his opponent was thinking ... he should have won.

---

[62] According to correspondence from Eisenbeiss to the author on 13 November 2006.

Sources
Invited Spirit Conversations

<u>Friends and Strangers</u>
Hodgson, Richard, "A Further Record of Certain Phenomena of Trance," *Proceedings of the Society for Psychical Research*, vol. 13, 1897-98, pages 295-334.

<u>A Mysterious Death</u>
Gay, Kathleen, "The Case of Edgar Vandy," by *Journal of the Society for Psychical Research*, Vol. 39, March 1957, pages 2-61.
MacKenzie, Andrew, "An 'Edgar Vandy' Proxy Sitting," *Journal of the Society for Psychical Research*, Vol. 46, September 1971, pages 166-173.
Keen, Montague, "The Case of Edgar Vandy: Defending the Evidence," *Journal of the Society for Psychical Research*, Vol. 66, October 2002, pages 247-259.

<u>New Meaning for "Soul Mate"</u>
Eisenbeiss, Wolfgang and Dieter Hassler, "An Assessment of Ostensible Communications with a Deceased Grandmaster as Evidence for Survival," *Journal of the Society for Psychical Research*, Vol. 70.2 No. 883, April 2006, pp. 65-97.
Neppe, Vernon, "A Detailed Analysis of an Important Chess Game: Revisiting 'Maróczy versus Korchnoi'," *Journal of the Society for Psychical Research*, Vol. 71.3 No. 888, July 2007, pp. 129-147.

Sir William Crookes

An esteemed British physicist and chemist, Crookes taught at the Royal College of Chemistry before becoming a meteorologist at the Radcliffe Observatory, Oxford. In 1861, he discovered the element thallium, and later invented the radiometer, the spinthariscope, and the Crookes tube, a high-vacuum tube which contributed to the discovery of the X-ray. He was founder and editor of Chemical News and later served as editor of the Quarterly Journal of Science.

Crooks was knighted in 1897 for his scientific work, and awarded the Order of Merit in 1910. A Fellow of the Royal Society, he received honorary degrees in law and science from Birmingham, Oxford, Cambridge, Ireland, Cape of Good Hope, Sheffield, and Durham universities.

In His Own Words:

"When I first stated [in the *Quarterly Journal of Science*, October, 1871] that I was about to investigate the phenomena of so-called Spiritualism, the announcement called forth universal expression of approval, [it was said] that 'if men like Mr. Crookes grapple with the subject, taking nothing for granted until it is proved, we shall soon know how much to believe.'

These remarks, however, were written too hastily. It was taken for granted by the writers that the results of my experiments would be in accordance with their preconception. What they really desired was not the truth, but an additional witness in favor of their own foregone conclusion. When they found that the facts which that investigation established could not be made to fit those opinions, why – 'so much the worse for the facts.' "[63]

---

[63] Crookes, Sir William, *Researches into the Phenomena of Modern Spiritualism*, Austin Publishing Co., 1922, p. 13.

Chapter Eight

Qualities Of Evidence

Of all the men professionally of science who have seriously and persistently investigated and studied the alleged phenomena of 'spiritualism,' the overwhelming majority have drawn the conclusion, as a result of their patient researches, that there is personal survival of death.

— Booth Tarkington[64]

W e were finishing some fine pasta at Mama Ventura's when he took a sip of his Chianti, sat his glass down on the checkered tablecloth, and asked:

"The cases at the end of *The Survival Files* are clearly more evidential of an afterlife than those that you described near the beginning, are they not?"

"Yes, I felt that you were saving the most impressive for your finale. But all of my readers haven't agreed with the order," I replied.

---

[64] Introduction to *Neither Dead Nor Sleeping*, by May Wright Sewall.

"Nor would I expect them to. Decisions that are entirely subjective will never be unanimous."

"Do you think," I wondered, "that it is possible to develop an objective way of evaluating the evidence for Survival?"

"We could give it a try," he said, pulling a pen from his pocket.

"I'll be happy to," I said, "but I'm not certain that my readers are going to be interested in such a dry subject as evidence evaluation."

"Oh, you can put the tedious stuff in an appendix," he said as he moved aside his empty plate, flipped over his placemat, and began writing. "But you ought to try and get the basic concepts across, because it's really important that people understand what makes good evidence and what doesn't."

"Well, there sure are a lot of books out there full of pretty weak cases."

"Then let's try to figure out what sort of occurrences are truly evidence of an afterlife," he said and he continued to write for a while as I stared through the front window, trying to imagine the streets crowded with Union soldiers instead of tourists.

In only a few moments, he interrupted my reverie with: "Let's start with a person who goes to see a medium. Assume that the medium doesn't know the sitter. She goes into a trance and tells the sitter these various things." And he handed me the list he had just written.

After I translated his scratchings, filled in the blanks, and cleaned it up a bit, the list looked like this:

- The name of the departed friend's fiancé, whom the sitter was not thinking about.
- That the departed friend had a brother who died in infancy; a fact the sitter had never known.
- Where the departed friend had hidden some money; a fact that no one else but the friend knew.
- The name of a departed friend from whom the sitter hoped to hear.
- That the departed friend's grave marker had been damaged by lightning the day before; a fact that was not known to any living person.
- The name of the departed friend's first dog, which the sitter had forgotten.

"Some people would say that each of these is proof of Survival, some would say none are. Some would admit one or more to be proof, but not all," he said. "Let's deal first with those who claim that none of these situations offer proof of Survival. They have only two arguments available to them. First, that the mental powers of the living are sufficient to account for the occurrences. Second, that the report was inaccurate or the phenomena fraudulent.

"Those who assume that all evidence must be the result of mistakes or trickery — even though they cannot discover the mistake or detect the trickery — are essentially taking a religious stance. Since nothing can shake their firm belief in the impossibility of Survival we can move on, leaving them to their cold devotions.

"Now, the idea that feats typically attributed to discarnate spirits are actually within the capabilities of the human mind deserves some attention. After all, we cannot be certain what the limits of the mind are."

"Yes," I agreed, "as far back as 1903, Myers wrote an excellent book[65] on that subject."

"Absolutely, but for those who posit powers of mind as an explanation for some, if not all, incidents indicating Survival, we should reiterate that the act of mental telepathy is, in and of itself, strong evidence for the existence of a non-physical plane of consciousness, and thus, indirectly, of Survival."

---

[65] Myers, F.W.H., *Human Personality and Its Survival of Bodily Death*, 1903.

He was referring to a conversation we had at his cabin, the gist of which was: It isn't so difficult to accept that we can mentally send and receive thoughts; the tough part is figuring out how a mind could sort through all the billions of thoughts that are being sent out at any given moment and read only the sought for message. The problem is not in the transmission or the reception, but in the tuning. Without some structure, all any mind could ever receive is the "white noise" created by the intermingling of the thoughts of every being in the universe. This argues strongly for the existence of some sort of universal mind or discarnate communications system that routes and delivers mental images according to our intention or desire. Such a system couldn't be limited to our own minds; it would have to exist in a mental plane independent of the physical.

> "In fact," he continued, "we can't be sure that there is any such thing as mental telepathy. The "Universal Mind" or "Cosmic Consciousness" required to properly route mental messages may, by itself, be sufficient to explain all mediumistic and psychic talents."

"Do you mean that all psychic phenomena could be the work of spirits?"

> "That doesn't seem likely, does it? But it seems more likely than the idea that all `spirit' effects are caused by mental powers of the living."

"It occurs to me," I mused, "that if we must choose between accepting that a bit of information was communicated from the mind of a spirit or that it was derived from the mental feats of the medium, our decision might hinge on just how difficult a task the medium would have had to perform."

> "I can go along with that," he agreed. "The more demanding and complex are the mental gymnastics necessary to garner the information or create the effect, the simpler, more rational, and intuitively easier it is to believe that a discarnate entity is the true cause."

"Well, then, looking at your list, the first thing that strikes me is that receiving thoughts seems an easier task than reading minds. If a sitter was concentrating on a large blue star, it would be somewhat impressive for a psychic to describe the star. How much more impressive it would be, though, if the psychic could also tell the color of the pajamas that the sitter wore the previous night. Even though both bits of data exist in the sitter's mind, I can accept the possibility of thought reception more readily that the ability to read the entire contents stored in another's mind. Therefore, if a spirit testifies to a fact on which the sitter was concentrating (such as the name of a deceased friend) the evidence for the spirit actually being that deceased friend is not as strong as if the spirit were to give the name of the deceased friend's fiancé which the sitter knows but was not thinking of at the time."

"Okay, we'll rank these in order of difficulty, with the simplest on top, and place the 'name' entry above the 'fiancé' entry." And he drew an arrow indicating that shift of position.

"Likewise, reading information stored only in someone's unconscious mind should be more difficult than reading the memories that they can normally recall. Thus, spirit testimony of a forgotten fact that resides only in the sitter's subconscious (such as the name of a deceased friend's first pet) is more evidential than giving a consciously remembered fact."

"So, we put the 'pet' entry below 'fiancé'," he said, drawing another arrow.

I was on a roll now, so I continued: "Research has shown that mental telepathy is not affected by physical distance; thus, the possibility that a medium might be reading the mind of a person across the country should be given no more weight than reading the mind of a person across the table. But relationships matter, even if proximity does not. The fewer connections that can be found between a medium or the sitter and the person whose mind contains the information, the less probable that mind-reading will be a satisfactory explanation. For instance, revealing a fact only known by people not involved in the sitting (such as the lost infant) is more evidential than giving facts known (consciously or unconsciously) by the people involved."

"You're saying that the information about the friend's deceased brother, if it didn't come from the friend's spirit, would have to have been pulled from the minds of the friend's parents."

"Yes, and their relationship with the sitter is weak or non-existent, so the medium, if she were not actually in contact with the spirit of the deceased friend, would face the herculean tasks of locating the friend's parents when there was no reason to do so nor any overt hint as to where they might be ... and then reading their minds to discover memories of a lost child."

"Of course, the medium wouldn't have to read both parent's minds; but having the ability to find and plumb even one is still incredible."

"True enough, but that makes me think of a situation you haven't described for our deceased friend. Sometimes the information received is only partially known by one person while the remainder is known by another."

"Okay," he said, "I'll place 'brother' beneath the 'pet' entry and add a line for 'multiple targets.'"

"So, now we come down to information known only by the spirit — the hidden money and the singed tombstone. Why did you make that two separate entries?"

"Well, you are correct that obtaining information only known by the spirit cannot be attributed to mental telepathy. But if the knowledge was possessed before death, some might claim that it became part of the Akashic Records or some sort of cosmic data bank and that the medium could access it there."

"I've always thought that to be a really big stretch."

"A really big stretch, indeed! Especially when the person propounding that theory also claims that individual minds do not survive the body's demise.

"Nevertheless," he continued as he drew more arrows, "the most powerful evidence of all is the reception of information that was uniquely obtained by a spirit after it left its physical body."

When he had finished, the list looked like this:

Relative Strength of Evidence (from weakest to strongest):

- The name of a departed friend from whom the sitter hoped to hear.
- The name of the departed friend's fiancé, whom the sitter was not thinking about.
- The name of the departed friend's first dog, which the sitter had forgotten.

- That the departed friend had a brother who died in infancy; a fact the sitter had never known.
- Information divided among two or more people's minds.
- Where the departed friend had hidden some money; a fact that no one else but the friend knew.
- That the departed friend's grave marker had been damaged by lightning the day before; a fact that was not known to any living person.

"You know, mental telepathy and cosmic data banks aren't the only alternatives. Some of my readers might think that clairvoyance or remote-viewing could account for discovering buried objects or observing stormy graveyards."

> He laid down his pen and said: "There is some evidence that remote-viewing, or whatever you want to call it, does work — sometimes; but successful procedures require that a target be consciously selected and then carefully concentrated on. If a skilled practitioner were given the coordinates of a particular grave, he might be able to 'view' it and report back as to whether the headstone appeared to have been struck by lightning. But even then, the ability to wend one's mental way through the vastness of the universe to a specific spot demands the existence of some sort of map and navigation system. So, we're right back to the requirement for a cosmic consciousness.

"Without being given a specific target, though, there is simply no way that a medium's mind, operating solo, could first sense that something had been struck by lightning, then identify what it was and who it belonged to, and then discover its placement. Such a feat could only be achieved with the guidance of someone who had observed the damage and knew the location."

"So, it's pretty clear," I summarized, "that mental telepathy, clairvoyance, and maybe other psychic powers could be the proper explanation for some evidence given for Survival, but they certainly cannot explain all cases."

"This is very true," he affirmed as he stood and brushed a scattering of crumbs from his ample stomach. "And since the spirit explanation must be accepted in some cases, then it is very likely a factor in most."

The Case of the Missing Information

We paid our check and walked . . .

"Okay, so we've got a good start on a way to objectively determine which cases make the best evidence for Survival. Trouble is, our approach is only useful for revelations of information."

Squinting in the afternoon brightness, he nodded: "This is true."

"So, what about incidents that seem to involve spirits but that don't have messages? The kind of events that are messages in themselves?"

"Do you have a particular one in mind?" he asked, halting to look into a shop window.

I didn't really, but when I stopped beside him I noticed, an angel figurine of hammered copper that was wedged between the wooden hearts and the plaques lettered with homespun aphorisms. "Well," I said, "there's that woman who was vacuuming and found an angel on her carpet.

"As I recall the story, she was in the habit of vacuuming her carpets weekly, and had done so many times since the Christmas ornaments were put away in the basement, when suddenly she almost ran over a golden angel in the middle of the living room. Unbeknownst to her, her husband had just discovered another angel lying on the basement floor. They agreed that the ornaments' appearance was the sign they had been seeking that their son had survived his body's death."

"Ah, yes. A most provocative tale."

"And famous too." I added. "I first learned of it when it was the subject of a segment on the *Unsolved Mysteries* TV show nearly a decade ago."

"Most believers no doubt think it's obvious that the appearance of the angels was just the sign that the parents were seeking, and was thus a powerful affirmation of the son's continued life in heaven."

"I gather you're not so sure."

"Oh, that might very well be the proper conclusion … but then again, it might not be. The problem is that we have no solid knowledge of how a spirit could manage such a feat. We do know that physical effects such as apports, rappings, and flying and falling objects seem to require the presence of humans (generally humans approaching puberty) but we have no idea what portion of the effect is typically caused by the human and what portion, if any, by a spirit.

"If the mind of a discarnate youth is capable of de-materializing a metal object from inside a cardboard box on one level of a home and re-materializing it on the surface of the carpet on another level, then would the minds of his living parents be any less capable? Is it reasonable to attribute certain powers to the dead yet deny them to the living?"

He stepped from the store window and turned down the street, letting his question hang in the air and giving me time to formulate an answer.

A block or so later I said: "Actually, yeah, I think there might be a couple of reasons."

"I'm glad to know the summer sun hasn't sapped all of your brain power," he said as he stepped into the shadow of a canvas awning. "What might these reasons be?"

"Well, for one, there are many cases in which the physical manifestations are used to transmit information. Rappings, table tilting, direct voice ... all these have a physical component. We have strong evidence that they are often associated with spirit forces. Therefore, it seems reasonable to assume that at least some of those manifestations that don't transmit information are likewise caused by spirits.

"Secondly, as far as I know, no one has managed to consciously perform telekinetic acts that show anything like the power and complexity of the typical poltergeist haunting — at least not in a laboratory. Yes, it might be possible for a mother or father to mentally teleport ornaments around their home, but such abilities are far beyond anything yet demonstrated. In fact, the only times that such extraordinary physical effects are reported are in cases where spirits are thought to be involved."

"You make some good points," he said. "You might also have reasonably claimed that the style of the ornaments chosen — angels rather than stars or icicles — was so appropriate to answering the parent's current concerns that it *was* information, although not verifiable information.

"Even so," he continued, "how do we rate such cases as evidence. Is an angel apport more evidential than a rainbow? Is it more difficult to psychically create sounds or to produce visual images? Is slamming a door a tougher trick than levitating a skillet?"

"I suppose we could develop some distinguishing criteria; but, since they each involve the movement of inanimate things — even a noise is just the movement of air molecules — we probably ought to simply rank all of them equally? Where we could make a distinction is between effects on living and non-living things."

"Which do you think are the more evidential?" he asked.

"Well, we generally consider mental telepathy to be more common than psychokinesis, so wouldn't it be more difficult to mentally influence a skillet than a hummingbird?

"I reckon it would. What about plants?"

"Ah yes, a lot of after-death communications do involve flowers blooming out of season or popping up where they were never planted," I noted. "I suppose that organisms without a brain would be more difficult to influence than conscious animals but easier to affect than inanimate matter."

"Seems like we're well on our way to another rating system. Why don't you write it up when we get back to the hotel?"

"I'll do that," I promised.

"And, while you're at it, you might want to share the `refrigerator' story with your readers as a good example of strong evidence for the presence of a spirit without the communication of information."

That I can do right here:

A Different Kind of "Cold" Case[66]

Promises to contact a living friend after one's death are often made but rarely kept. Even rarer are those that are fulfilled in a way that provides solid evidence of Survival.

In the final days of her battle with cancer, Mary Jasen made such a promise to her friend Christina. They had been friends for several years and Christina took Mary seriously, even though Mary's proposed method for announcing her spirit presence was a bit unorthodox. She said that she would knock loudly on the refrigerator to get Christina's attention. When Christina asked why the refrigerator, Mary jokingly pointed out how much she loved food and said that the

---

[66] See *Love Beyond Life*, by Joel Martin and Patricia Romanowski (pages 96 - 100) for the full presentation of this case.

refrigerator was her "favorite place." Then she told Christina to keep their arrangement a secret between them. A few months later, Mary passed on, and Christina awaited the signal.

Some five years later, Christina had pretty much given up any hope of hearing from Mary. Then, she had a dream in which she saw Mary and Len, who was Mary's husband, sitting at a picnic table in an unfamiliar park. In the dream, Mary turned toward Christina and said that she was fine and no one should worry about her. This was not the contact that Mary had been wishing for, but it made a vivid enough impression that, the next time she visited Len, she described her dream to the widower.

Len was more impressed with the dream because the park that Christina described was exactly like an area where he and Mary had often eaten lunch. This revelation lifted Christina's spirits, but the next thing that Len said was far more astonishing. A few days before, Len related, he had been in his kitchen when he had been startled by a banging sound as if rocks were being thrown at his windows. He could discover no culprit; but, when the sounds were repeated, he realized that the noises seemed to be caused by some unseen visitor banging loudly on the refrigerator door. He was perplexed but did not feel fear. In fact, he said that he somehow knew that his wife's spirit was responsible for the disturbance and he felt comforted.

If Mary's husband had dreamed of a picnic with his wife at a familiar location, no one would consider it indicative of anything — except, perhaps, that he loved his wife, or that he went to bed hungry. The fact that Christina dreamed of an area she had never visited is certainly suggestive, yet telepathy could explain it and unconscious knowledge cannot be ruled out. But if she had not had the dream, Len would not have been encouraged to tell Christina about the rapping sounds.

In almost every case of alleged spirit rappings, the evidential value comes from the information communicated, not the means of communication. This is because we cannot be 100-percent certain that living humans have less psychokinetic power than deceased humans. But, such an explanation simply doesn't wash in this case. If Christina's unconscious mind were going to generate loud raps on a refrigerator door, it would no doubt do so on her own appliance, not on that of someone who would not understand the significance of the disturbance. And, the husband is not a feasible source of the noises, as he was unaware of the friends' pact. This sort of "cross correspondence" leaves us with either accepting Mary's spirit as the source or conjecturing a psychic communication between Len and Mary, and vice versa, that triggered a psychokinetic outbreak by the unconscious mind of a 68-year-old man. In this case, Occam's razor is greatly in favor of the spirit explanation.

Touched By The Past

Wandering among the cannon balls, belt buckles, and tattered uniforms in the next shop on the street, we stopped to examine some coins, both Union and Confederate. "Looking at old coins often makes me think of psychometry. Wouldn't it be great to be able to read their history just by touching them?"

"Oh, I don't know," he replied. "I have enough trouble handling the sense impressions of the here and now. Can't say that I would appreciate being constantly bombarded by the then and there of everything I bumped into."

"As I recall, King Midas had a similar complaint," I mused. "But, if one could control it, what an entertaining and educational talent to have!"

"Or what a depressing talent," he replied. "Does not your study suggest that the impressions one can obtain seem strongest when linked to powerful, and usually negative emotions? To what horrors might these coins be linked? More than 30,000 soldiers were seriously wounded at Gettysburg alone; uncounted legs and arms were amputated (without anesthesia), thousands of young men deafened, or blinded, or paralyzed for the rest of their lives. No, as far as I'm concerned, these coins and all their siblings and cousins can keep their anguished history to themselves."

For a long moment, neither of us spoke as our minds skirted the edges of the intolerable sadness of civil war.

He turned toward the shop door. "Unfortunately, terror and suffering are much more likely to fill a psychometry session than peace and joy."

"But how does psychometry fit into our picture of the world and the afterlife?" I wondered. "How could it work?"

"Goodness! my young friend. You surely don't think that I have the answer to that?"

But, I just followed him out into the sunshine and said nothing.

"I doubt that any resident below the seventh heaven actually comprehends how such things work. If I may quote one of the first researchers into the paranormal, even advanced spirits can never `understand the hidden sphere of cause.'[67] "

---

[67] Robert Hare, *Investigations of the Spirit Manifestations*, p. 95. The full statement is: "Although advanced spirits are much more conversant with the forces operating in nature than the most intellectually developed man in the form, still they do not, nor can they ever, as long as eternity rolls on, understand the hidden sphere of cause."

I maintained an expectant stillness. ... He snapped a pair of shades over his steel rims and turned his steps back to our hotel. ... I followed quietly.

We hadn't even reached the end of the block when he broke the silence. Turning towards me with a resigned grin that I took as confirmation that he was aware that I knew that he could not resist any opportunity to speculate on such deep subjects, he said, "But if I *was* going to speculate on the workings of that hidden sphere, I would say that the best analogy we have for the universe would be a stupendously large and powerful computer network. Each conscious being is a tiny node in an almost infinite network of consciousness. And, at some level, every node is connected to, and can share information with, every other.

"So, I don't consider it useful to assign any consciousness or even memory to inanimate objects. When a psychometrist focuses on a coin or other object, he or she can trace the links through the network to the mind or the memories of others who have possessed it." With that, we hurried our steps towards the hotel, for the lunch break was almost over.

As we sat in the conference room awaiting the inevitable stragglers, he pointed to a program item concerning super-ESP and said softly, "You know, there is a counter argument to the super-ESP theory that we haven't mentioned yet. Those who deny the existence of independent spirits usually claim that mediums get their information by tapping into the minds of the living."

I nodded my agreement.

"Why then, would the information virtually always be about dead people? If we picture the medium somehow traveling around in mental space, picking up impressions that people have of each other, then shouldn't at least half of those impressions be about living persons?"

"Well," I said, "sitters don't generally pay mediums to provide information on folks that are still alive."

"A valid point. But what about 'drop-in' communicators?"

"You're referring to those entities that neither the medium nor the sitters know, who interrupt a session for reasons of their own? Like the captain of that English blimp?"

"Ah, yes. few drop-ins are as well known as Flight-Lieutenant Irwin, but you don't have to crash a dirigible to crash a séance. Unexpected strangers might make their presences felt whenever and wherever the living attempt to contact the dead. And, in almost every case, those strangers are not current residents of this earth. If Survival is erroneous and super-ESP is the true explanation, then those drop-ins should be representations of living people at least as often as they are of the dead."

"Not bad," I said, "not bad at all. Is this something you came up with?"

"No," he replied, "I first came across it in an academic paper. But I do take credit for digging it out of the middle of a 36-line footnote on the 56th page of that paper."[68]

"Well, I've got several good cases involving drop-in communicators; this will give me a fine intro."

---

[68] Gauld, Alan, "A Series of 'Drop In' Communicators," *Proceedings of the Society for Psychical Research*, Vol. 55, July, 1971, pages 273-340. Remarkably, the old man had the page and line numbers correct.

Talking To Strangers

You and I may not have the power to bring about sensational happenings, but at least we can, in our small way, help in the furtherance of the knowledge that there are vast horizons quite beyond our perception, stretching limitless into the infinite.

— F.W.H. Myers via G. Cummins

These three cases involve information given by a spirit previously unknown to anyone involved in the séance. These are generally considered to be more evidential than when information is supplied from a spirit that is somehow linked to the medium or the sitters.

The Rationalist Spirit
[Case ID# 46, ESS Score = 259, Current Rank 33rd]

In 1959, Dr. Alan Gauld participated in seven meetings of a "home circle" in Cambridgeshire, England. This group consisted of a few core people and assorted visitors who gathered in a private home to attempt contact with the spirit world, mostly via the talking board. The group met, with various participants, on and off from

1937 to 1964. Careful records were kept of the majority of the circle's sessions. Based on these records and a great deal of personal investigative work, Gauld produced a report titled "A Series of 'Drop In' Communicators." The term "drop-in" refers to spirits who are strangers to anyone in the circle and who arrive uninvited. Such intrusions are thought to be especially evidential because of the presumed difficulty of any participant reading the information from the mind of a person whose identity and whereabouts are unknown.

This case is of special interest because it reveals a rude and belligerent spirit; it is of even more interest because it shows a rude and belligerent spirit transforming into a polite and friendly one. To best demonstrate these characteristics, the dialogue is given verbatim, with the exception of a few irrelevant passages marked " * * * ". The comments in [brackets] are Gauld's, those in {braces} are my attempts to clarify a passage.

A note on voice and formatting: The messages spelled out on the board are printed here in a different typeface. "Peter" was a frequent spirit presence who served as a kind of control or astral traffic manager for the circle. Comments in normal (serif) typeface generally come from a male observer referred to as "R.W." but occasionally other members interject a comment. In the opening lines, Peter is referring to a session held by some of the participants in another home a few days previously.

['Peter' writes:] A little later I am going to let the eel slip through. He slipped along on Thursday [i.e., at the previous sitting] so I kept control. Stanley [R.W.'s deceased brother] and son will help me. Stan will help you son. Talk to him.

Is it a man, then?

Yes. Humour him. Get to know him. We can then deal with him from here – big job. We do not know him so I am wanting to make contact through you. Humour him. Thank you all – I am leaving now. No worry. No harm.

{At this point, the new spirit is allowed to take control.}

M.p.m.p. {meaningless?} I know all the ladies. {The spirit recognizes women in the group from the previous session.}

What is your name?

Lady I am Molly.

How can we help you?

I am helping you. You like me to talk. I help the ladies but kind Nell [Mrs D.] does not like me. She says I am Elsie [i.e., Miss E., Mrs D.'s customary partner on the ouija board].

You are helping both ladies?

Yes. I do and I bring them lots of people.

What makes you come to them? What is your job?

Talking.

You know you are on the spirit plane?

Yes. I am.

Why do you come to these ladies?

They wanted people from here. I am all the people really.

It must be hard to be all those people at once?

I am only one at a time.

Then you find you change from one to another?

Yes. Do not really change.

What is your real name, do you remember?

Yes. I will not say.

We want to help you.

I do not want your help.

But we would like to help you.

Why?

Because we are taught to help those who need it.

Wrong teaching.

I have a feeling you are a man.

I was happy with the ladies and I am not going to be bloody well pally with you. Mind your own business. I did not come to talk to you. Shut up.

[Mrs. W.G.] What is your name?

Mollie.

You spelt it differently a little while ago.

Rats. My friends talk to me.

[R.W.] I'm going to talk to you.

Mind your bloody business.

You must take your business elsewhere and not worry these dear people. Surely you don't use language like that to your lady friends.

Men friends.

What sex are you?

>Mollie.

Can you see anyone standing near you?

>Yes. Man.

Well, that is my brother and he is a good chap. He will help you.

>No. I cannot pretend here.

Isn't it better not to pretend, but to be yourself?

>You know a hell of a lot.

Do you remember your earth life?

>Yes.

What was your business?

>Not yours. I was a man who always kept to himself.

Oh, so you are a man?

>Damn. Like lady. Do you like religion?

Yes, but not over fond of it. Do you?

>Bloody rot.

That's only your opinion. You will be happier if you will be yourself and stop all this nonsense.

>Don't you talk. Let the ladies. I don't damn well like you.

I don't mind that, we want to stop you worrying our friends.

>Go now.

You will not go.

>I go.

Be reasonable.

Shut up, buggar you.

There are people who will help you.

Only Hitler can help. He is the master mind.

What is your real name?

What has that to do with you? Shut up blast you. I am going.

There is only one master mind, God, and you cannot alter that.

You make me sad. Go away.

I'd rather make you pleased.

Keep quiet.

I want you to promise to stop worrying our friends here.

Sorry.

That's better. That's the reply of an intelligent man, which I am sure you are.

I go now.

Go with the thought of friendship from us.

Shut up.

Go where you will, but be intelligent.

I come with my heart full of love.

You certainly do not, what do you take us for? What you are doing is a cad's trick.

* * *

You are not to worry our friends any more with your pretence. There is a Power which will stop you. You are afraid of it. That Power protects them.

Pray until your head falls off. I am German and my name is Gustav.

That's a French name.

Liar. You are mad. Gustav German.

What is your surname?

You say you help. I am Gustav Adolf Biedemburg. If I come and say Gustav would you like me better?

Not until you are sincere. Go with my brother, he will help you.

Will he like me?

He will help you.

I am not pretending about German.

What made you come to us? Why not to a German circle?

I lived in London. It is better as myself. You welcome me.

You may come again if you first ask permission of the greater power, Peter or Bob.

I must ask greater power first.

Yes, that's the idea.

Yes. I am myself now.

Did you pass in air raid?

No. My house was Charnwood Lodge.

What address?

Let me think for next time I come.

Ask Bob and Peter to help you.

I am going now with a kind friend who will listen and talk.

Give that friend my kind regards.

['Peter' writes:] Many thanks son.

Was he really sorry?

Yes and he is German.

January 7, 1943

[Operators: Mrs W.G. and Mrs G.J. Recorder: L.G. Also present: R.W.]

I offer my humble apologies and add to them my grateful thanks.

We are only too glad to have been of help. Come when you like, you will find friends here, and Mrs D. and Miss E. will welcome you too.

I want to help. I am not lonely now. I will tell you my correct name. Adolf Biedebmann. I always was known and called Gustav.

Shall we call you Gustav?

Please. I was a rationalist.

What exactly is that?

A type of religion to follow only the reasoning of one's own mind. It puts a barrier around.

That is why you have been so lonely and found no companions?

Yes. Partly.

* * *

I had my own business.

What was it, do you remember?

No. In some remote way I am associated with the
Lond[on] University.

When did you pass over?

Year ago

Was your business a bookshop?

No.

Publishers?

Rationalist Press.

Do you want to remember your earth life?

Yes. I am happy though. I am forgiven for my
lapse?

Yes, of course, it was no fault of yours.

Thank you all. Goodnight.

In investigating this case, Gauld discovered no
"Biedemburg" or "Biedebmann" but changing only
one letter gives "Biedermann" and there can be no
doubt that is the name the spirit attempted to communicate. Dr. Adolf Gustav Biedermann was a Ger-
man-born, naturalized citizen of England who lived at
Charnwood Lodge on the outskirts of London until he
died at the age of 73. He was a fairly wealthy businessman who also worked in the Psychology Department at London University.

Those who knew Biedermann described him to
Gauld as an arrogant, obstinate, and aggressive man
who, nevertheless, could be a pleasant companion
when one got to know him. He seemed to revel in his

German heritage and never dropped his accent. One acquaintance portrayed him as "an out-and-out rationalist" who may well have been attracted to the idea of Aryan superiority. Biedermann once wrote a sarcastic letter to the London Times about experiments on telepathy. His disdain for religion is demonstrated by his will, which instructed that his children be brought up without any religious instruction whatsoever, and that he himself should be cremated without any religious ceremony. Also in this will, Biedermann bequeathed money to the Rationalist Press Association.

A spirit using crude and aggressive language is not unheard of, but it is rare and does not seem to have occurred at any of the other sessions held by this home circle. Thus, it cannot reasonably be attributed to either of the operators.

Case 69: The Murder of Jacqueline Poole
[Case ID# 39, ESS Score = 277, Current Rank 7th]

The gruesome slaying took place on the 11th of February 1983. The killer was identified within a few days. He was tried and convicted 18 years later.

The delay was not the fault of Ms. Christine Holohan of Ruislip Gardens, West London.

Holohan called the police in response to their broadcast request for information that could shed light on the murder of a bar maid named Jacqueline Poole. Although Holohan had never met the victim in life and knew none of her family or friends, she had read something about the crime in the local paper and she had a feeling that the presence she had been sensing might be the spirit of Poole. When it actually appeared to her, however, the spirit identified herself as Jacqui Hunt.

The different name than that published in the media was the first thing that got the attention of Police Constable Tony Batters when he and Detective Constable Andrew Smith called on Holohan a day or so later. But the knowledge of Poole's maiden name was only the first drop in a flood of information supplied by her spirit via Holohan. Poole's spirit had come to Holohan for justice, and she provided 131 separate facts concerning her murder. These included:

- On the evening she was murdered, Poole was supposed to go to work but did not because she felt ill.
- Two men had come by intending to take her to work.
- After they left, another man came by to visit her.
- She knew this man through friends, but she did not care for him.
- She let him into her flat.
- She thought he had a message for her from her boyfriend.
- Her boyfriend was currently in detention.
- When the police arrived at Poole's flat, there were two coffee cups visible in the kitchen. One clean and one with coffee remains.
- Also visible were a black address book, a letter, and a bottle of prescription medicine.

Holohan went on to describe the attack, struggle, and murder in what the police referred to as graphic details, but those details were not released to the public. She said that there were rings missing from the body. Furthermore, she mentioned five names associated with the victim: Betty, Terry, Sylvia, Barbara Stone, and Tony.

Because Constable Batters had been the first on the scene of Poole's murder, he was aware of the coffee cups, address book, and other such details of the location. Of the other facts transmitted via Holohan, all but 10 were verified by the time the case was closed, and all but one of those were consistent with the known facts. The single at-variance item was Holohan's mention of Sunday, from which it was inferred that she thought the murder to have taken place on Saturday rather than on Friday.

"Betty" was Jacqui Poole's mother. "Terry" was her brother. "Sylvia" was her boyfriend's mother. "Barbara Stone" was a friend of Poole who had died several years previously, but the police did not make the connection at the time.

As for "Tony," when Holohan tried some automatic writing in her attempt to name the murderer, the only person's name she wrote was "Pokie." The constables immediately recognized that as the rather uncommon nickname of one of their key suspects, Anthony (Tony) Ruark.

Ruark, who had a history of criminal, but not violent, behavior, had already been interviewed by the police; however, no solid evidence of his guilt could be found. Based on Holohan's revelations, the man was detained and grilled at length and various items were confiscated during a search of his home. Nevertheless, no incriminating evidence was uncovered and Raurk was again released.

With nothing further for the police to go on, the Jacqueline Poole case grew cold, and what items had been collected as possible evidence were placed in storage. There they remained for 18 years until an informant claimed knowledge of the killer and the investigation was reopened. As it turned out, this new informant named the wrong man, but in the process of going over the stored evidence using the latest in DNA technology, the truth was revealed. A pullover that had been taken from "Pokie's" trash was found to have skin cells, body fluids, and clothing fibers that conclusively linked him to the murder.

In August of 2001, Anthony Ruark was convicted of Poole's murder and sent to jail for the rest of his life. Justice for Jacqui Poole was delayed, but her efforts to communicate via Holohan were not in vain, for it seems that it was the medium's prolific and accurate statements that triggered the search of the killer's home and resulted in the collection of the damning evidence. If that contaminated shirt had not been found in

Ruark's trash, he would most likely have remained a free man.

The typical case in which mediums claim to have helped the police has little corroboration from the police themselves. Poole's murder investigation is most uncommon in that the detectives involved agreed to be interviewed by the researchers, supplied the researchers with copies of their original notes, and signed statements[69] affirming the accuracy of the researchers' report on which this article is based.

Psychic detective work is not, of course, the focus of The Survival Top 40. Therefore, the issue here is not how impressed the police were, but whether or not Holohan could have obtained her information from sources other than Poole's discarnate mind.

Some critics have claimed that it is not impossible for Holohan to have obtained her information through normal means. When each fact is considered separately, their arguments make some sense ... sometimes. For instance, it is possible, as one critic suggests, that Poole's father, who was allowed access to the murder scene momentarily to identify the body, happened to

---

[69] Declaration: I confirm that the above account agrees with my recollection of my interview with Christine Holohan and with my knowledge of the case. (Signed) Anthony Paul Batters. Metropolitan Police Warrant No. 153617. 27.11.2002; (Signed) Andrew Smith, Detective Sergeant. Metropolitan Police Warrant No. 91/167901. 27.11.2002.

pry his eyes away from the mangled body of his daughter long enough to note that there were two coffee cups sitting out in the kitchen. It is also possible that he felt the necessary curiosity and had the presence of mind to examine these cups and determine that one was clean and one still had some coffee in it. And it is just possible that in his grief-stricken state he thought to describe these cups to someone else. And, yes, it is possible that that someone was sufficiently impressed by two innocuous coffee cups to pass on the information and that — somewhere down the line of gossip — "news" of the cups reached Holohan. Possible ... but extremely unlikely.

To posit a long string of such outlandish possibilities for scores of other trivial facts is either being disingenuous or downright silly.

And then there are the facts that Holohan simply had no way of knowing, such as the name of Poole's deceased girlfriend, Barbara Stone. Even the police didn't make that connection for nearly 20 years.

Other critics might claim that Holohan was gleaning the information via mental telepathy. The coffee cups and such she could have pulled from Constable Batter's mind; the murder details from Ruark's mind; knowledge of the two who came to escort Poole from their own minds, and so on. Pulling just the relevant facts from so many different minds is theoretically possible ... say, about as possible as winning the lottery ten times in a row. But even those willing to swallow the idea of such super-ESP must choke on Holohan's mention of Barbara Stone — a girl who had nothing to do with the murder and wasn't even alive at the time.

The one mistake that Holohan possibly made actually strengthens her credibility, because the one thing that everyone involved in the case knew was that Poole was killed on a Friday. If Holohan was such a brilliant weaver of lies and guesses, she surely wouldn't have been wrong about the day of the week. Discarnate spirits, on the other hand, generally display a poor comprehension of time and dates.

Fire and Iceland
[Case ID# 39, ESS Score = 277, Current Rank 7th]

It took 103 years for the facts about the Jensen case to fully emerge … the wait was totally worth it!

The name Indridi Indridason might seem strange to most readers, but for a period of five years, this young man was the best-known medium throughout his native Iceland. So varied, prolific, and amazing were the manifestations of his power that a special committee of highly respected professionals was formed to study him.

The committee was called The Experimental Society and its 70-plus members included a professor of theology at the University of Iceland and a newspaper editor who later became Prime Minister of the country. In addition, Dr. G. Hannesson, an honored scientist who was appointed Professor of Medicine at the University of Iceland, studied Indridason over several months. Despite his initial skepticism, Hannesson concluded by stating his "firm conviction that the phenomena are unquestionable realities."[70]

So meticulous was the Experimental Society that they had a house designed and built in Reykjavik that featured living quarters for Indridason and a secure hall for séances. The hall was generally filled with up to 100 observers, even though attendance was by invitation only. Much of his mediumship was physical (involving lights, levitations, and such) but there were some mental phenomena, i.e. information presented from inexplicable sources.

The most written about mental phenomena of Indridason's brief career concerned a spirit who told the séance audience about a fire taking place in Copenhagen. This took place on November 24, 1905, and, on their own, do argue strongly for the Survival hypothesis. Information uncovered in 2008, however, raises the case to an entirely different level.

In brief, the events of 1905 unfolded as follows. Around 9 p.m. the medium began to speak as a spirit claiming to be a deceased man named Jensen who said that he had been to Copenhagen and observed a fire raging in a factory there. About an hour later, Jensen

---

[70] Hannesson, Gudmundur, "Remarkable Phenomena in Iceland," *Journal of the American Society for Psychical Research*, Vol. 18, 1924, p.29.

came through once more and stated that the fire was under control.

Three of the witnesses have given public testimony to these facts and, within a day, a record was entrusted to the Bishop of Iceland to keep until these statements might be confirmed. Copenhagen is about 1300 miles distant from Reykjavik and, at the time of the séance, there was neither telephone nor telegraph service between the two cities. It was thought that the fire might be reported in a newspaper when it arrived by ship from Copenhagen.

When the paper did arrive, it contained a story confirming the four facts given in the séance. There was one large fire in Copenhagen on the night of November 24th. It was in a factory on Kongensgade (a main street). It had been reported about the time given by Jensen, and was brought under control in about an hour.

Many commentators have remarked on the similarity with the famous report of Swedenborg's announcement of the great fire in Stockholm (in 1759) while he was visiting Gothenburg, some 245 miles away. Swedenborg, did not claim that that specific piece of information came from a spirit, only that he had seen a vision, so his experience is not evidential of Survival. Also, there was a strong connection, at least theoretically, between the fire and the seer, as the fire consumed the homes of several of Swedenborg's friends and was not extinguished until it had almost reached his own. No such connection was apparent between Indridason or Jensen and the fire on Kongensgade — at least no connection was realized at the time.

The hand-written records of Indridason's séances filled many large volumes, all of which were presumed lost for the past half-century. In 1991, however, two of the missing volumes were discovered in the estate of a former president of the Icelandic Society for Psychical Research. Even so, it wasn't until another 17 years had passed that a professional researcher carefully examined these records. Dr. Erlendur Haraldsson[71], the author of numerous books and papers on psychic phenomena, calls his unexpected discovery "perhaps the most memorable finding of [my] life."

Scattered among the thousands of notes in these records are several, hitherto unknown, facts about the earthly life of Mr. Jensen, including that:
• His first name was Emil.
• He was a manufacturer.
• He was unmarried and childless.
• He died when he was "not young."
• He had several siblings.
• All of whom outlived him.

Haraldsson tried to corroborate these statements by combing through old business directories, census

---

[71] Professor emeritus of psychology at the University of Iceland.

data, and birth and burial records at the Royal Library, the National Archives, and the City Archives in Copenhagen — and he was 100-percent successful!

Here is what the professor discovered:

- There was one, and only one, Emil Jensen listed as a manufacturer in Denmark (despite Jensen being one of the most common surnames in the country).
- This Emil Jensen lived almost his entire life within a few blocks — much of the time within a few yards — of the factory that burned.
- He never married.
- He had no children.
- He died at age 50.
- He had four sisters and two brothers.
- All of whom died after 1905.

Between his report of the fire and his statements about his personal life, we count 12 distinct facts stated and confirmed by the spirit of Jensen, and no statements contradicted or challenged by careful research. This is made all the more convincing by the physical isolation of the séance from Copenhagen, the direct connection between Jensen and the location of the fire, and the lack of any link between the séance attendees and the events described or the participants therein.

We are left with no feasible conclusion other than that the spirit of Emil Jensen detected a serious fire near his earthly residences and immediately communicated that news via the most accomplished medium holding a séance at that hour.

Sources
Talking To Strangers

The Rationalist Spirit
Gauld, Alan, "A Series of 'Drop In' Communicators,"
Proceedings of the Society for Psychical Research, Vol. 55,
July, 1971, pages 273-340.

The Murder of Jacqueline Poole
Playfair, Guy Lyon and Montague Keen, "A Possibly Unique
Case of Psychic Detection," *Journal of the Society for
Psychical Research*, Vol. 68, no. 874, January 2004, pp. 1-
17.
Holohan, Christine, *A Voice from the Grave: The Unseen
Witness in the Jacqui Poole Murder Case*, 2006 (Listed here
as pertinent although not consulted for this write-up.)

Fire and Iceland
Haraldsson, Erlendur, "A Perfect Case? Emil Jensen in the
Mediumship of Indridi Indridason, the Fire in
Copenhagen on November 24th 1905 and the Discovery
of Jensen's Identity," *Proceedings of the Society for
Psychical Research*, Vol. 59, October 2011, pp. 195-223.

Cesare Lombroso

Lombroso obtained his doctorate in medicine from the University of Turin and became a neuro-psychiatrist. Then served as an army physician. In 1862, he was appointed professor of diseases of the mind at Pavia, then took charge of the insane asylum at Pesaro. Later became professor of medical law and psychiatry at Turin. The son of a long line of rabbis, Lombroso founded the Italian School of Positivist Criminology and is considered a key originator of the science of criminology.

In His Own Words:

"If ever there was an individual in the world opposed to spiritism by virtue of scientific education, and I may say, by instinct, I was that person. I had made it the indefatigable pursuit of a lifetime to defend the thesis that every force is a property of matter and the soul an emanation of the brain."[72]

"I am ashamed and grieved at having opposed with so much tenacity the possibility of psychic facts – the facts exist and I boast of being a slave to facts. There can be no doubt that genuine psychical phenom-

---

[72] Lombroso, Cesare, *After Death – What?*, Small, Maynard & Co., 1909, p. 1.

ena are produced by intelligences totally independent of the psychic and the parties present at the sittings."[73]

[73] Fodor, Nandor, *Encyclopaedia of Psychic Science*, University Books, 1966.

Chapter Ten

The Darkness Dialogue

There are no miracles that violate the laws of nature. There are only events that violate our limited knowledge of the laws of nature.

— Saint Augustine

The grand conference room of the Gettysburg hotel was once the lobby of an elegant bank. There are chandeliers hanging from the intricate tray ceiling and, near the current entrance, a massive door guards the opening to the bank's now-empty vault. Sitting near that steel behemoth, while awaiting the start of the next session, the old man and I shared a few thoughts about what a neat setting the vault might provide for a séance. Would the tons of steel and concrete deter the spirits? There certainly would be no problem restricting access, or achieving the total darkness that so many spirits seem to require.

"I note," he said, "that the system by which you propose to rank cases for the Survival Top 40 excludes any incident that is not sufficiently illuminated to be observed clearly. Do you think all of the reports from darkened séance rooms are fallacious?"

"It isn't what I think that matters," I replied. "As you know, the Top 40 are supposed to be the cases that are most likely to convince the reader that we do live on. Since most folks, quite rightly, are suspicious of what might occur under cover of darkness, I am reticent to include such cases, even if I have no reason to suspect fraud."

"But have you ever considered that total darkness can reveal as well as hide?"

"No. Can't say that I have."

"Well, consider that if you've been sitting in the dark for a long time so that your eyes are as well adjusted as they can get and you still can see absolutely nothing, then anyone or anything that moves easily and precisely about the room must possess inhuman powers of sight.

"We have testimony from scores of participants in hundreds of pitch-dark séances that something intelligent was capable of moving about rapidly without bumping into any furniture or person. Likewise, many sitters have spoken of being deftly touched, tapped, and even kissed in a way that no human could duplicate without sufficient illumination. In addition, comments revealing a clear view of the room are often made by seemingly disembodied voices."

Later, I retrieved this passage from Findlay's *On the Edge of the Etheric*[74] in which he is discussing sittings with the medium John C. Sloan:

"[A spirit] reprimands someone for sitting with his legs crossed, which is one of the first things a novice at a séance is told not to do. The novice, thinking that as we are sitting in the dark no one will see him, sometimes disobeys this injunction, but forgets that the darkness is no darkness to them, that they see us clearly, and everything we do. A tap by the trumpet on the culprit's head, and a polite request not to cross his legs, invariably proves this; in fact, I have never known a mistake to be made. ... Other instances have occurred, quite apart from the regular voice phenomena, to show that the etheric intelligences present can see in the dark. I shall mention a few.

"At the close of a sitting, just before the farewells are said, I have often held out my watch and asked the time, and on every occasion, when the lights have been turned on, I have found the reply correct almost to the minute, and this be it remembered is done in the dark and when no luminous watches are in use. This correct time telling, moreover, occurs after a sitting of from two to three hours. Again, if I hold my finger in any direction it

[74] Findlay, Arthur, *On the Edge of the Etheric: Or Survival After Death Scientifically Explained*, 1931, pp. 135-136.

will, on request, be gently touched with the trumpet; no fumbling, a clean gentle touch. Any part of
the body, on request, will be cleanly and gently
touched, either ear, the nose, the left or right
knee—an impossible thing, as I have proved, for
any human being to do in the dark."

And all this long before the invention of night-vision
goggles.

"Furthermore," my companion pointed out, "there
is another aspect of darkness that argues for the
reality of spirit intelligences. That is the impossibility of a medium carefully studying a sitter's
demeanor and posture in order to seemingly read
her mind. As Findlay states, `It might be possible
for a human being with the deductive faculty of a
Sherlock Holmes to have some idea of our
thoughts in daylight, from a study of our facial
expressions, but in the dark, never.'[75]

"Finally, the inability of séance participants to
see in the dark sharpens their aural acuity and
eliminates visual cues that could be misleading.
The right clothing, a pair of spectacles, maybe
even a beard, in dim light, combined with the desire to believe, can result in a false recognition. But
the voice alone is not so likely to be misidentified.

---

[75] *Ibid.* p. 173.

"To us, darkness is blindness. If spirits see 'with their minds' then everything would seem to be illuminated whether or not there was any light present."

Even though I do not plan to eliminate the requirement for clear observation from the Top-40 ranking system, I see the validity of these points, and so include them here for further consideration by both researchers and skeptics.

Not Seeing Is Believing

Cases that depend upon eyewitnesses are, of course, seriously weakened when the witnesses cannot see clearly. But, when the medium or percipient is blind-folded or otherwise in the dark, the evidentiary value can be greater. The best examples of this effect are probably cases involving the "Ouija" board.

Boards covered with letters and numbers that could be pointed to with a small triangular table known as a "planchette" or "traveler" were often used by spirit seekers during the early 1880s. On February 10, 1891, Elijah J. Bond was granted the first patent on such a board. His business partner, Charles Kennard gave their version the name "Ouija," which he falsely believed was Egyptian for "luck." Parker Brothers bought the rights to the name in 1966, so I will use the generic "talking board" from here on.

Of all the diviner's devices, the talking board is the most popular. Perhaps this is because its low cost and ease of use appealed to many who wouldn't think of buying a crystal ball or learning to read tarot cards. Also, using the board is a social thing requiring at least one person and usually two people to touch the traveler and another to copy down the messages being spelled out. Before the advent of horror movies on late-night television, many young folks sought answers to burning questions ("Will I marry a handsome man?" "Does Frankie love me?") from the board. This proved especially thrilling on dark and stormy nights amid flickering candles.

Unfortunately, not all encounters with the powers behind the board have been so innocent or harmless. Many people claim that playing with a talking board can open portals to other dimensions, letting in immoral or amoral spirits who revel in encouraging nasty deeds and may even try to possess the naive planchette pusher. The recommendations made for dealing with such interlopers range from prayer to envisioning white auras to trashing the board altogether.

Nevertheless, the talking board is hugely important because several of the best mediums and channelers employed it to make their initial contact with the spirit realms.

This author would, therefore, advise those trying out the talking board to exercise caution and common sense. Any messages coming through the traveler should be evaluated in the same manner as would commentary or advice received from any other stranger. As the Bible commands, "Do not trust any and every spirit, test the spirits to see whether they are from God."[76]

Skeptics are quick to claim that the only thing coming through talking boards is the inner self of the user and that the results are either fantasy or repressed memories. These critics are often correct; but when the operators have no link to the information sources, the evidence is very convincing. And it gets even more convincing when the operators are kept in the dark as to the location of the letters.

The Honorary Secretary of the S.P.R. for Russia, Michael Solovovo wrote an article describing how a certain Lieutenant Colonel Starck obtained previously unknown information while ensuring that the operators of the board could not be influencing the messages. Prior to each session, Stark would bandage the eyes of both women so that they could see nothing. Then he would write the letters of the alphabet in random order on a piece of paper and place it on a table between the women. He would next place their hands on the traveler — in this case, a small over-turned saucer with a pointer attached. As he asked questions, the traveler would move quickly and precisely to spell out the answers.

---

[76] 1 John, 4:1. See Appendix One for more on the Biblical injunctions regarding speaking with spirits.

A similar approach was used by the Unitarian minister, Dr. Horace Westwood. This is his description of how his 11-year-old daughter, Anna, got started with the board: "So we let them try, one by one, and each pulled a blank, much to their chagrin, until Anna placed her little hand on the planchette. She had hardly touched it, when the indicator began to move with startling rapidity and with equally startling accuracy, spelling out words and sentences in complete and intelligent sequence." Turning the board around had no effect on Anna's remarkable ability, nor did blindfolding the girl. The next day Westwood drew the letters of the alphabet "higgledy-piggledy" on a large piece of paper. "Indeed," he explains, "they presented such a confused picture that if I wanted to spell out any word, and with my eyes wide open, it was an effort to find the letters." Such precautions proved pointless. When Anna was blindfolded and led to the scrambled board, the tumbler flew just as rapidly and the messages came just as intelligently as before.

One of the most inventive and certain methods of preventing operator input was devised by a circle of friends in Dublin, Ireland. They created a board consisting of letters on individual cards that could be arranged in any order. This display was then covered with a sheet of glass 22-inches square. The various arrangements had no effect on the rapid movements of the traveler or on the precision with which it spelled out meaningful messages. Neither did blindfolding the operators have any deleterious effect; nor did placing opaque screens between the blindfolded operators and the board. In other words, there was absolutely no way that either person touching the traveler could have any idea — via their normal senses — of what letters were being pointed to or what messages were being spelled out. Often, in fact, the operators distracted themselves with light talk and laughter even when serious messages of disaster or despair were being communicated through their darting fingertips.

In each of the three situations described above,[77] the message(s) contained accurate information unknown at the time to anyone involved. But it should be emphasized that the ability to rapidly spell out *any* meaningful message when the location of the letters is hidden is, of itself, strongly indicative of spirit influence.

---

[77] For details on this and the preceding two descriptions, see case numbers 49, 67, and 40 at SurvivalTop40.com.

Conversion Phobia V

Horace Westwood

Born in Yorkshire, England, Westwood became an ordained minister of the Methodist Episcopal Church in 1906 and pastored at Sault Ste. Marie, Michigan. In 1910 he joined the Unitarian Church and was pastor successively at the First Unitarian Church, Youngstown, Ohio; All Soul's Church, Winnipeg, Manitoba, Canada; and First Church, Toledo, Ohio. He was minister at large for the Unitarian Church (1927-33) and for the First Unitarian Church, Berkeley, California, ending his career as pastor of the oldest Unitarian church in the South, in Charleston, South Carolina. He was the author of 20 books on religion and morality.

In His Own Words:

"To be concerned with the question of individual survival beyond death when there is so much misery and suffering upon earth is the essence of selfishness."[78]

"The entire thing is utterly foreign to the world of fact I think I know. Also, it leads to an outlook upon life which I regard as inimical to the best interest of mankind. Such a possibility is entirely beyond the

---

[78] Westwood, Horace, *There is a Psychic World*, Crown Publishers, 1949, p. 9.

range of any consideration I could entertain, even for a moment."[79]

"I am scientifically convinced that thought and personality can manifest themselves apart from a brain and body as we now conceive them. This I hold to be true, because the phenomena upon which the inference is based can be repeated ... they are verifiable."[80]

"I am convinced that the truth of immortality may ultimately prove itself to be the only cornerstone upon which a decent and humane society can really depend."[81]

---

[79] *Ibid.*, p. 3.

[80] *Ibid.*, pp. 196-197.

[81] *Ibid.*, p. 199.

Spirit Possessions

From the moment that I had understood the overwhelming importance of this subject and realized how utterly it must change and chasten the whole thought of the world when it is wholeheartedly accepted, I felt … that all other work which I had ever done, or could ever do, was nothing compared to this.

— Sir Arthur Conan Doyle[82]

Possession, for our purposes, involves the apparent take-over of one person's body by the spirit of a deceased person without the living person's knowledge or consent. The possession may last only a few minutes, or go on for weeks, or even for as long as the possessed body remains alive.

The "Deadicated" Reporter
[Case ID# 66, ESS Score = 261, Current Rank 30th]

The description of events given below was written out by A.A. Hill, of New York City, and published by businessman and researcher Isaac Funk (the publisher

---

[82] Carr, John Dickson, *The Life of Sir Arthur Conan Doyle*, Barnes & Noble Books, 1994, p. 268.

of the Funk and Wagnalls dictionaries). Mr. Hill was known to Funk and described by him as a man of character and intelligence. At the time he wrote the story – at Funk's urging – Hill was the editor of *The Amateur Sportsman* magazine.

"Some twelve or fifteen years ago, I was the editor of the *New York Sunday Dispatch*, a newspaper well known at that period and for many years before.[83] One of our reporters was a man named Williamson, a son of the former owner, then deceased. He was about thirty years of age, and having long been connected with the paper, was retained on the staff by the new owner, more because of his faithfulness and loyalty and out of respect for his lamented father, than because of his journalistic or intellectual ability. It was his duty to take care of the city fire-department news and gossip, and his interest in the fire department and its affairs was unusual – I could almost say, phenomenal. Moreover, if to his faithfulness and zeal for his work had been added average talent, he would have been a treasure as a reporter. It used to wound his feelings greatly whenever I found it necessary to curtail or otherwise edit the copy he turned in concerning what seemed to me to be rather trivial fire-department matters.

[83] One well-known contributor to this paper was poet Walt Whitman.

"But he was suddenly stricken with illness and died within a few days. In casting about for someone to fill his place, I bethought myself of a quiet, modest, but very bright young journalist who had previously been in my employ in another city. In engaging him I was careful not to inform him that a member of the staff had died or that he was to fill a vacancy. The position did not warrant paying a large salary, and a bright young man could take on other work. So I wrote my young friend that I could find work for him if he would come on and be willing to do anything called upon to do. He arrived the following Wednesday afternoon, and being a stranger in the city, I met him at the railway station and took him to the office. I gave him the desk formerly occupied for a good many years by his predecessor, who had then been dead for about a week, telling him he need do nothing that day, and if he would excuse me for a time while I finished some writing, I would then take him up-town and find him a place to board.

"In about fifteen or twenty minutes he suddenly appeared at my desk, looking astonished and agitated. He laid two sheets of manuscript before me, written on the usual copy paper of the office, with the remark: 'I did not write that.' I could not see much sense in the remark, but replied: 'Well, if you didn't, who did? Some of it looks like your handwriting.' His reply was: 'I don't know; as soon as I sat down I never felt so peculiar and drowsy in my life. I must have gone to sleep and when I was awakening I found myself writing, but it doesn't all look like my handwriting.'

"Now, I should explain that this young man's handwriting was nervous, small, and not clearly legible, while his dead predecessor had written a large, round hand that could be read easily. But the writing in question varied between that of the two; some of it was like the writing of the dead man and some like that of the new reporter, and other parts of it were a composite or intermixture of both. The last few words were undecipherable, and the sentence was apparently unfinished. It should likewise be stated that the deceased reporter had for years begun his report of the meetings of the fire commissioners in this form: `The regular weekly meeting of the fire commissioners was held last Wednesday, Commissioner in the chair.' The manuscript the young man had placed before me began that way, altho if he himself had been the author of it in his normal condition, it would by no means be the form he would begin a newspaper story of that kind. It purported to state what had been done at a fire commissioners' meeting, and altho it was not all clear or complete, there was enough to puzzle me.

"Now comes the most singular fact: I preserved the two pages of manuscript, and the next day ascertained what had been done at the fire commissioners' meeting, held perhaps an hour or two before it had been written. I was astonished to find that, so far as it went, it was a correct report of what had actually taken place.

"What was the agency by which this information was conveyed? Was it thought-transference or mind-reading? It could not have come from me. I certainly neither knew nor cared what they did at the meeting, and I had intended to omit publishing the report for that week altogether, or get an abstract for publication from some other paper, not sending the new man for the report until the following week. The information could hardly have been 'thought transferred' by any living fire commissioner from another part of the city; none of them was especially anxious that the Sunday Dispatch publish their reports, even if he were able to thus 'project' the information through space in this way. It could have been no one in the newspaper office, for no one had such information to impart, and there was only an office boy and a bookkeeper on the floor. It could not have been any trick or duplicity on the part of the new reporter himself. He knew nothing about the fire commissioners, or their meetings, or that they were published in the paper which was to employ him, even tho he had possest the miraculous power of reporting a meeting several miles away and when not attending it.

"Could the man who had just died, and who had always taken such a vital interest in the fire department and in the reports in the Sunday Dispatch concerning these meetings, have returned in spirit and through the new reporter communicated the report for publication?

"I will leave the solution to the reader. I have only stated the absolute facts."

Being that these events took place over a hundred years ago, it's easy to assume that they are somehow less valid than cases described in more recent books, but on close examination, the evidence for Survival presented here is quite strong. Anyone who has read Isaac Funk's works could have no doubt of his integrity and perspicacity. Hill correctly points out that telepathy offers no enlightenment. Some might fall back on other extra-sensory explanations, but there was no link between the new reporter and the meeting's venue – no path for a mind, or thoughtform, or whatever to follow. So the theoretical possibilities of clairvoyance, an OBE, or remote viewing just aren't feasible. Also, the new reporter had neither the means, motive, nor opportunity to trick his new boss, even if he were crazy enough to try. The absolute facts that Hill has so succinctly provided point directly to the Survival of the human personality and to naught else.

The Return of Mary Roff
[Case ID# 45, ESS Score = 270, Current Rank 14th]

Teenage girls are the focal point of many strange stories. What makes this tale really weird is that it involves two girls, both teenagers, who were born 12 years apart.

Although she was often a loved and loving child, from the time she was six-months old Mary Roff had been afflicted with seizures that gradually increased in violence. As she grew into a young woman, Mary started hearing voices and began to complain of a "lump of pain" in her head. To relieve her headaches, she would repeatedly draw out her blood with leeches. Whatever was causing her agonies seemed also to bestow psychic powers, as it was claimed that she could read sealed envelopes and closed books while tightly blindfolded. She became known throughout her hometown of Watseka, Illinois, and her alleged powers are said to have been carefully investigated by prominent citizens, including newspaper editors and clergymen.

Mary's special talents could not save her, however. After slicing her arm in an apparent suicide attempt, she was committed to a mental hospital, where she died on the afternoon of July 5, 1865, at the age of 18.

Some 12 years later, another girl named Mary, living at the other end of the same town, began showing similar symptoms. There were two main differences between the Marys. For one thing, this second girl was named Mary Lurancy Vennum, and she was known as Lurancy or simply "Rancy." For another, Lurancy had seemed perfectly healthy until she was nearly 14. Then one day, July 11th, 1877, to be exact, Lurancy had some sort of seizure and lost consciousness for five hours. A similar episode occurred the following day, except that the seemingly unconscious girl began speaking of seeing dead people. This sort of thing happened several times daily for the ensuing six months, leading many friends and family members to suggest commitment to an asylum. No doubt these suggestions would have been followed, were it not for the interference of Mary Roff's father.

Since the death of his daughter, Mr. Asa Roff had sat with a couple of mediums, had received material he thought came from his daughter, and had come to believe in the existence of a spirit world. Furthermore, he suspected that sending his daughter to an asylum had been a mistake. When he heard of the tribulations of Lurancy, Roff was concerned that the same mistake might be repeated. So, he contacted the Vennum family – with whom he was distantly acquainted – and persuaded them to allow a friend to try and assist the girl.

Roff got considerably more than he bargained for.

The friend was Dr. E.W. Stevens of Janesville, Wisconsin, who was skilled in hypnotism. Stevens traveled to the Vennum home in Watseka and Roff introduced him to Lurancy in the presence of her family. Much of what we know about this case comes from material published later by Stevens, although others also did follow-up investigations.

When Stevens first saw Lurancy she was sitting in a chair with the posture of an old hag. He drew-up a chair and she savagely warned him not to come nearer. She identified herself as a woman named Katrina Hogan and she was reticent and sullen, but she said she would talk to the doctor because he was spiritual and would understand her. Then, suddenly, that personality was gone and she claimed to be a young man who had recently run away from home, gotten into trouble, and lost his life. Finally, Stevens managed to induce a hypnotic trance and "was soon in full and free communication with the sane and happy mind of Lurancy Vennum herself." She claimed that she had been influenced by evil spirits but that now there were angels around her and one of them wanted to come to her. On being asked if she knew who it was, she said: "Her name is Mary Roff."

Mr. Roff, although surprised, naturally thought that was a great idea. He encouraged Lurancy to let Mary come through, saying that his daughter was good and intelligent, and would be likely to help Lurancy since she used to suffer from a similar affliction. Lurancy, after seeming to discuss the matter with her attending spirits, agreed that Mary would take the place of the former wild influences.

Mr. Roff, apparently thinking that Lurancy would now be in control with Mary's aid, said to her: "Have your mother bring you to my house, and Mary will be likely to come along, and a mutual benefit may be derived from our former experience with Mary." But, the next morning, the first day of February, 1878, the girl who awoke in Lurancy's bed and body claimed to actually *be* Mary Roff. She showed no recognition of the Vennum home or any of the family members. She just wanted to go home "to see her pa and ma and her brothers."

The next day, there was no change; nor the day after that. Mrs. Roff and her daughter, Mrs. Minerva Alter (Mary's mother and sister) came to see the girl at the Vennum home. As they came in sight, far down the street, "Mary"[84] spied them from a window and exclaimed, "There come my ma and sister Nervie!" – the name that Mary had called her sister in their childhood. For over a week, although she remained docile and polite, "Mary"constantly pleaded to go "home" and showed no signs of leaving Lurancy's body. Finally, on February 11th it was agreed that she could go and live with the Roff family. This was not intended to be a permanent arrangement, though, as "Mary" said that

---

[84] To minimize confusion, the name Mary (printed plainly) indicates the original Mary Roff and the name "Mary" (in quote marks) indicates the apparently possessed Lurancy Vennum.

she would only be allowed to remain in control until "some time in May."

And so, for the next 14 weeks, the Roff's were visited by a person who, except for her physical appearance and the lack of seizures and despondency, was in every way the daughter they had lost over 12 years previously. "Mary" immediately recognized every relative and family friend that Mary had known since infancy. She always called them by the names that Mary would have been familiar with; but she treated the Vennum family as total strangers.

These affirmations of her true being started on the way to the Roff home across town. As they traveled, they passed by the house where they had been living when Mary died. "Mary" demanded to know why they were not returning there and they had to explain that they had moved a few years previously.

She proved herself familiar with hundreds of incidents, both major and trifling, that had occurred in her previous life; sometimes spontaneously and sometimes in response to careful questioning. She knew what articles of clothing belonged to Mary and which ones Mary had made. She knew exactly where her brother was scarred when a stovepipe fell on him. When asked if she remembered a certain dog, she immediately pointed out the precise location in her sister's home where it had died. Never did any statement, or way of talking, or gesture give the slightest hint that she was not who she claimed to be.

"Mary" was thoroughly familiar with the horrid "treatments" that Mary was subjected to in attempts to cure her supposed insanity. She remembered cutting her arm, but when she started to pull up her sleeve to show the scar, she suddenly stopped and said, "Oh, this is not the arm; that one is in the ground." She then spoke of watching her own funeral and of sending messages to her father during his séances and she gave the exact times and locations of those sessions and correctly repeated the messages transmitted.

And then, around 10 o'clock on the night of the 20th of May, "Mary" came down from her sleeping quarters and lay down with Mr. and Mrs. Roff, hugged and kissed them and wept, saying that she must leave them again. The next morning, after bidding goodbye to her friends and neighbors, "Mary" was driven by the Roffs back to the Vennum home. By the time they arrived, Lurancy was back in control of her own body, where she remained, whole and healthy, until her death in the late 1940s.

A Country Revival
[Case ID# 71, ESS Score = 275, Current Rank 9th]

This story concerns two women, Susan Singer[85] and Sharon DeMint, who lived about 60 miles apart and

---

[85] All names in this discussion have been changed for reasons explained later.

never met or heard of one another prior to the occurrences detailed here.

Singer was raised on a tobacco farm near Owingsville, Kentucky. She never attended school, picked up her very basic reading and writing skills from a friend, got married at 15 to Jacob Singer, moved into his parent's home and, 3 years later, gave birth to a son.

In contrast, DeMint's father was a college professor in Berea, Kentucky, and she took advantage of the complementary tuition to get her bachelor's degree in home economics. She was married at 18 and had two sons.

Only 6 months after the birth of her second child, on the 19th of May, DeMint's dead body was discovered lying between the tracks of the local railway.

One of DeMint's uncles had visited her the evening before and reports that she had been crying over mistreatment by her in-laws, but that she had not seemed suicidal. DeMint's father accused her in-laws of murder, but a police investigation failed to find compelling evidence thereof. No doubt this failure was partly due the fact that her husband had her body cremated immediately, so there was no way to confirm eye-witness testimony that the corpse did not appear to be mangled as would be expected if hit by a train.

A few months prior to DeMint's rather suspicious demise in Berea, Singer began to suffer periods of loss of consciousness that lasted from a few minutes to an entire day. On two occasions she was seemingly possessed briefly by discarnate personalities. One of these claimed to have been a local Owingsville woman who had drowned herself in a well; the other asserted that he had been a man from Muncie, Indiana.

Although the ministrations of a local healer did seem to calm Singer at times, they did not stop her intermittent trances. During one mid-summer episode, she predicted her own imminent demise, and 3 days later she seemed to have achieved that state. Her respiration and pulse were undetectable and her face became drained of blood like that of a dead person. A considerable group of persons surrounding her were convinced that she had died, and some began to cry. There was no doctor available to make a declaration, so we'll never know whether or not Singer was clinically dead. All we know is that, when she revived several minutes later, she recognized neither her surroundings nor her family. She said little or nothing for a day after her revival. Then she announced that her name was Sharon DeMint, and she demanded to be taken to her two sons in Berea. By that time, the actual body of Sharon DeMint had been naught but a pile of ashes for nearly two months.

Singer's in-laws thought that she had become possessed by a wandering discarnate personality who could be exorcised away or might leave spontaneously as had previous ones. But they made no attempt to verify that any such person had ever lived in Berea. Whatever efforts they made to banish the invading personality were clearly failures as the spirit of Sharon DeMint remained in control of Singer's body for 13 years, until she died – or died again.

It took a month before DeMint's father got wind of a story about a young girl claiming to be his deceased daughter. On October 20th, he traveled to Owingsville and tracked down the girl, who immediately recognized him as her father.

These incidents soon caught the attention of the press, and folks sent clippings from two different newspapers to the best-known investigator of such cases, Dr. Ian Stevenson. Within a month, Stevenson and his colleagues began interviewing witnesses. Over the next three years, interviews were conducted, and re-conducted, with 24 family members and another 29 folks who were in a position to furnish background information, especially concerning the communities and the intercourse between them. About 22 years later, a follow-up investigation was done by other researchers that involved interviewing some 15 surviving witnesses and examining a couple of previously unavailable letters that Singer/DeMint had written to DeMint's father. Rarely, if ever, has an apparent case of possession been so thoroughly investigated.

The pertinent facts these researches revealed are:

• All those who were part of, or had knowledge of, Singer's family testified that they had no previous acquaintance with DeMint's family.

- All those who were part of, or had knowledge of, DeMint's family testified that they had no previous acquaintance with Singer's family.
- When DeMint's father heard a rumor that his dead daughter had taken possession of a girl in Owingsville, he did not even know where the town was located.
- The revived Singer/DeMint (hereinafter referred to as "DeMint"— in quote marks) had knowledge of several of DeMint's possessions, including a particular yellow dress, and a watch and the box in which it was kept .
- "DeMint" knew the respective order of birth of DeMint's maternal uncles (although one who was younger actually looked older than one of the older uncles).
- "DeMint" knew which two colleges DeMint had attended.
- "DeMint" knew both of DeMint's pet names (as used by her family) and the names of her two children, two brothers, two of her sisters, two of her maternal uncles, a maternal aunt, and a nephew.
- When DeMint's father showed "DeMint" a photograph taken 18 years earlier, she correctly identified all six persons, including "herself," saying "This is me."
- "DeMint" was equally accurate in identifying the people in several other photographs, none of which had ever been available to the public or the press.

- In one of these photographs, she identified DeMint's sister-in-law, describing her additionally as the person "who hit me with a brick."
- On the other hand, "DeMint" recognized no member of the Singer family and none of the locations in which Sharon Singer had lived.
- Letters written by DeMint and "DeMint" were analyzed by a handwriting and fingerprint expert who concluded that there was "an overwhelming preponderance of probabilities that these letters have been written by the same person."
- Although Singer had virtually no education and could barely write, "DeMint" demonstrated a degree of literacy and knowledge one might expect from a college-educated spirit working through an unfamiliar body.
- Once she awoke, it soon became apparent that "DeMint" was unaccustomed to having to leave the house to relieve herself. Unlike the Singer home, the DeMint home had indoor toilets.

The number of witnesses, the number of researchers, and the number of facts presented, combine to make this a most convincing case for possession. Some might argue that it does not add to the proof for Survival after death because the spirit of DeMint was operating not from the grave but from a living body. The proper rejoinder to that is to ask: Where was the spirit of Sharon DeMint during the two months between the time her body was cremated and the time she awoke in the body of Susan Singer?

*   *   *

As stated in the initial footnote, the names of the people and locations described in this case have been changed. The reason for this is rather unusual; it wasn't done to protect anyone's privacy, but to facilitate comprehension of the facts of the case. The events described took place in India, not Kentucky. The research papers from which this case was derived used, quite naturally, the actual names of the people and villages involved. The strangeness of these terms to my English-educated ear and eye greatly increased the effort required to sort out who did what to whom and where. On the assumption that others might face the same resistance to absorbing the facts — and thinking that this difficulty might explain why the case has not been more widely recognized — I took the step of "translating" the names into those more easily digested by western readers. I certainly do not mean to denigrate the ancient and honorable languages of the Indian sub-continent. Neither, by the way, do I mean to suggest any ill regard for the people of Kentucky. In fact, my maternal ancestors were from the areas mentioned and I choose Owingsville to honor the memories from visiting there in my youth — tobacco fields, outhouses, and all.

Sources
Spirit Possessions

The "Deadicated" Reporter
Funk, Isaac, *The Psychic Riddle*, 1909, Class V, Case 1.

The Return of Mary Roff
     The case was first published in 1879 as "The Watseka Wonder" in the *Religio-Philosophical Journal*, and published in pamphlet form in 1887 titled *The Watseka Wonder: A Narrative of Startling Phenomena Occurring in the Case of Mary Lurancy Vennum*, by E.W. Stevens.

     Additional evidence was obtained by Dr. Hodgson in personal interviews with some of the chief witnesses and printed in the same journal in December 1890.

     The editor of the journal, said by F.W.H. Myers to be well known as a skillful and scrupulously honest investigator, endorsed Stevens and claimed that great pains were taken before and during publication to "obtain full corroboration of the astounding facts from unimpeachable and competent witnesses."

A Country Revival
Stevenson, Ian, Satwant Pasricha, and Nicolas McClean-Rice, "A Case of the Possession Type in India With Evidence of Paranormal Knowledge," *Journal of Scientific Exploration*, Vol. 3, No. I, pp. 81 - 101, 1989.
Mills, Antonia and Kuldop Dhiman, "Shiva Returned in the Body of Sumitra: A Posthumous Longitudinal Study of the Significance of the Shiva/Sumitra Case of the Possession Type," *Proceedings of the Society for Psychical Research*, Vol. 59, Part 233, October, 2011.

Sir William Fletcher Barrett

Barrett lectured on physics at the Royal School of Naval Architecture before becoming professor of physics at the Royal College of Science in Dublin in 1873. He taught there for 37 years, retiring in 1910. Knighted in 1912.

Barrett developed a silicon-iron alloy used in the development of the telephone and transformers, and did pioneering research on entoptic vision, leading to the invention of the entoptiscope and a new optometer. He was a fellow of the Royal Society, Philosophical Society, and Royal Society of Literature as well as a member of the Institute of Electrical Engineers and the Royal Irish Academy.

In His Own Words:

"In a paper I read before the British Association in 1876, [I wrote] that where fraud did not explain these physical phenomena, and the observers were men of unimpeachable integrity ... the witnesses thought they saw what they describe, owing to mal-observation or some hallucination of the senses such as occurs in incipient hypnosis. In fact I began the whole investigation of these phenomena convinced that this was their true explanation"[86]

"It was not until after stretching this hypothesis to illegitimate lengths that I found the actual facts completely shattered my theory"[87]

"I am personally convinced that the evidence we have published decidedly demonstrates (1) the existence of a spiritual world, (2) survival after death, and (3) of occasional communication from those who have passed over."[88]

---

[86] Barrett, Sir William, *On the Threshold of the Unseen*, E.P. Dutton & Co., 1918, p. 37.

[87] *Ibid.*, pp. 37-38.

[88] Barrett, Sir William, *Death-Bed Visions*, The Aquarian Press, 1986, p 162.

Chapter Twelve

Angels Or Aliens?

"Unfortunately, those interested in flying saucers had no interest at all in psychic phenomena, and vice versa. Those who were busy trying to trap a Bigfoot frowned upon all other forms of the weird and supernatural. Yet sea serpents, Abominable Snowpersons, poltergeists, frog rainfalls, and UFOs are all interrelated. You can't possibly investigate one without some knowledge of the others."

– John Keel[89]

McClellan's Tavern looks just like it's name suggests, subdued lighting on the imported mahogany bar and frosted glass on the doors. They likely served the same beer here as anywhere, but it somehow tasted especially good on this night. Perhaps it was the friendly crowd and the even friendlier bartender that heightened our appreciation, or maybe it was the satisfaction of capping off a most productive day, sitting on a comfortable leather stool

---

[89] Quoted from a publication of the New York Fortean Society, 1991, excerpted in *Fate*, September 2007, page 12.

beside a good friend. We had just ordered our second round of summer ales when I overheard someone sitting at a small table behind me make a comment about the "weirdoes invading the place next week." At first, I was taken aback and started to wonder if I should be insulted, then I remembered seeing a placard in the lobby announcing an upcoming conference on UFOs. Apparently the old man heard the comment also.

"The most salient thing about the psi/UFO connection," he said, "is that virtually no one involved wishes to recognize it. There is hardly any intercourse between the 'angels-are-real' community and the 'aliens-are-real' community."

"Perhaps this is because each is convinced of their subject's authenticity and dubious of the other's," I speculated. "Each is fearful of being tainted by too close an association — as if their truth would somehow become less true if the other were found fallacious."

"This fear of contagion is not uncommon among groups on the fringe of society. Take nudists, for example. Instead of 'hanging together lest they be hung separately,' many nudists (not all, by any means, but many) are intolerant of any deviation from society's norms, except, of course, lazing around the pool in their birthday suits."

"Don't tell me you're against social nudism."

"Oh no!" he replied. "I always say that if God had wanted people to run around naked, He would have made them that way."

Once I figured out what he meant, I replied: "But, that's a two-edged sword. You could just as well say that if God had wanted people dressed, He would have inspired them to make clothing."

"But of course! God wants to experience both states — that, you may recall, is what this old world is all about: God experiencing being Himself through us. And that is why all preferences should be kindly tolerated." He took a sip from the glass just set before him, wiped a bit of foam from his beard and added, "… except, of course, a preference for intolerance."

"So you don't think that the investigation of angels and aliens should be kept separate?"

"There certainly is value in focus;" he stated, "nevertheless, I believe much benefit could be derived from investigating where and why the two fields overlap."

Common Factors

"The first thing that comes to my mind, is that both UFO and psychic phenomena seem able to affect electrical and electronic equipment."

"Yes. This is so common, in fact, that lights, radios, engines, and other devices turning on and off 'by themselves' have become clichés in the literature of both groups. If the witness is at home, such phenomena will likely be interpreted as ghostly; if in an automobile, flying saucers will likely be blamed, especially if strange lights appear in the sky.

"And strange lights," he continued, "are likewise construed to be either angels or aliens depending upon where they manifest. A ball of light swooshing through one's bedroom will generally seem mystical, while one outdoors will probably trigger thoughts of cosmic invaders."

"Unless," I pointed out, "the out-of-doors phenomena occur over a cemetery … at midnight … on Halloween."

"Ah yes," he grinned, "expectations are always important.

"Perhaps the most striking effects shared by psychic and UFO manifestations involve the apparent utilization of other dimensions. Ever since our previous meeting, I have been thinking of these as 'twink links.' "

[Author's note for those who may not have perfect recall of that conversation: We commented that it is possible that our universe rapidly blinks into existence and out of existence and that other universes or dimensions exist within our 'off' moments. Such multiplexing could help explain many otherwise inexplicable phenomena. In that earlier conversation, I suggested that 'twinkles' was a better term than 'blinks,' so he now refers to each 'on' period as a 'twink.']

"There are at least two possibilities here," he continued. "The first seems to involve a time displacement in which persons suddenly find themselves in another world. They may experience this alternate reality for only a few brief moments or for what seems to be several hours. However long they stay away, the length of time they experience in that place is not congruent with the time that has passed in this world. It is as if they were re-created in the wrong dimension where they stay until the 'mistake' (if such it was) is discovered and they are then re-inserted into their proper world, but not quite at the proper twink. Reports of such incidences are not common, but they're not all that rare either. Whether or not they are interpreted as the work of spirits or spacemen (or fairies) is pretty much a matter of who is doing the interpreting.

"A second type of event is more of a space displacement than a time warp. Often termed 'teleportation,' this phenomenon involves something or someone disappearing from one place in our physical world and reappearing instantaneously (or almost so) in another physical location. When people are involved, they generally have no sense of time passing, so that one moment they are in one location and the next moment they are somewhere else. Again, the twinkle paradigm would suggest that the teleportee somehow was de-created at one place and re-created at a far different location."

"I'm not sure I can buy this twinkle thing," I said, "even if I did come up with the name."

"Well, whatever the truth may be, I think such metaphors are useful in helping us grasp some very real phenomena. Both time and space displacements have been reported numerous times in both UFO and psi literature."

I took out a pen and started jotting notes on a cocktail napkin. "It strikes me as rather unlikely that the same sort of experiences are actually caused by different factors," I said. "So, either a lot of supposedly psychic occurrences are the result of alien technology or many UFO encounters are really spiritual events."

"Or there is some common bond between the two that we have yet to fathom." he added.

"Another commonality between spirit entities and space entities is the postulate of other planets and planes being occupied by souls. If we answer the questions: 'Where are these beings coming from and how do they travel from one plane or planet to another?' for aliens, we may well answer for angels also."

"You don't mean that heaven is up-there, somewhere, in outer space?"

"Probably not. The hypothesis that would explain most observations is that both angels and aliens travel extra-dimensionally rather than that both reside in Alpha Centauri. But further research is definitely needed on the matter.

"Another strange characteristic of both spirits and spaceships is that they are sometimes seen in photographs but not by the naked eye. In almost all cases of ghostly images and many cases of shiny disks appearing on negatives, the photographer was unaware of anything unusual when the shutter clicked. Investigators really should give more consideration to the differences between the sensitivity of camera film and the human retina."

"Most of the so-called 'ghost pictures' that I have seen are just fuzzy blobs and streaks of light," I said.

"Yes," he agreed, "but have you noticed that the figures in many pictures taken with early cameras back in the 1800s are much more clearly delineated?"

"I always assumed that those were simply fakes."

"You should examine the evidence closely before judging them all so harshly. If you did, I believe you would conclude that many are not so easily dismissed."

"Why would photographs taken with antique cameras register ghostly forms more clearly than modern equipment?"

"I've been considering that very question," he replied, "and I'm wondering if it might have more to do with the lenses than with the film emulsions."

"But, early cameras had much simpler lenses, some little more than pin-holes."

"What if the energy that is imprinting the ghost images onto film is not 'light' as we normally think of it? What if this energy — call it 'ghost light' — was capable of affecting film emulsions but was not as easily refracted as light waves? That would mean that the lenses that focus the light would have little or no effect upon such emissions so the image of the ghost or spirit would register on the film but would be blurred."

"I see what you mean. A pin-hole camera (having no lens at all) would cast regular light and this 'ghost light' equally well onto the film plane. But the more complex the lens, the larger the difference between the focused regular light and the less refracted ghost light.

So, earlier cameras and simpler cameras could be better tools for ghost hunters than more advanced ones."

"It does seem an idea worth further investigation," he concluded, "but we probably ought to get back to the subject at hand."

[Comments added later: Upon reading over my notes of this conversation, it occurred to me that there is another major difference that could possibly account for the clearer images in early photographs – the length of the exposures. Today's cameras, both film and digital, take pictures in a small fraction of a second; in the 19th century, taking a picture indoors without a flash could require exposures of 15 minutes or more. Could it be that the qualities of our speculative "ghost light" require extra long exposures despite today's improved sensors?

I also wonder if the partial transparency of many ghostly appearances might result from the spirit only being manifested intermittently – say every third twink or so.]

"Okay," I said, referring to the scribbles on my napkin, "so far we have seven areas of overlap between survival research and UFO investigations: electronic effects, mysterious lights, temporal displacements, spatial displacements, place of origin, means of travel, and photographic effects. Any others?"

"Two that I can think of right now," he responded. "The first is the fact that animals often react strangely in the presence of both psi manifestations and UFO visitations. Brave dogs are often known to cower and hide; cats hiss at the air, cattle panic, and so on. Frequently, these occurrences are a human's first hint of an unusual presence.

"The other similarity that comes to mind is that both spirits and spacemen claim to be the source of channeled messages to us earthlings. The number of mediums who claim psychic contact with physical beings from other star systems is much smaller than those who seem to speak for discarnate spirits, but there have been a few."

"I think that Uri Geller once made such a claim."

"Yes, he asserted that aliens from a far distant planet called 'Hoova' were the source of his psychokinetic powers ... Of course, this sort of talk didn't make him any points with parapsychologists. The überskeptics loved it, naturally, as they could easily avoid dealing with Geller's phenomenal abilities by throwing up a screen of derision centered on the 'little-green-men.'

"But Geller is not the only psychic to connect with beings claiming to be aliens rather than angels. Ken Carey and Lenora Huett are two that come immediately to mind."

Reciprocal Recognition

"Speaking of communications, are there any channeled teachings that touch on the subject of UFOs?"

> "I'm hardly familiar with all the information that has ever come from the mouths of mediums, but I do recall that Roberts had something to say on the subject, and Walsch also."

[Note: I looked it up later and found his memory accurate. The Seth entity, channeled by Jane Roberts, made several statements about the reality of non-Terran civilizations and alien craft, including, "I am quite sure — I know for a fact — that beings from other planes have appeared among you, sometimes on purpose and sometimes completely by accident."[90] The origin of these beings, he claims, may be physical or non-physical.[91] For those readers concerned about invasions, it may be reassuring that Seth does not believe we "will have any saucer landings for quite a while" [because] "These vehicles cannot stay on your plane for any length of time at all."[92]

As for Neale Donald Walsch, a fair portion of Book 3 of *Conversations with God* is devoted to the characteristics of various cultures throughout the galaxy.

---

[90] Roberts, *The "Unknown" Reality, Volume Two*, p. 754.

[91] Roberts, *Seth Speaks*, p. 473.

[92] Roberts, *The "Unknown" Reality, Volume Two*, p.755.

Walsch's 'god' claims that there are thousands of civilizations more advanced — and a much smaller number less advanced — than ours.[93] Furthermore, he states that such highly evolved beings refrain from directly assisting mankind because humans tend to worship them as gods.[94] If so, then they must have visited earth in the past.]

"We haven't covered past-life regressions," I pointed out. "Do subjects under hypnosis ever speak of living lives as aliens?'

"It's pretty rare, but it does happen enough to rate mentioning. In his life-between-lives regressions Dr. Michael Newton has encountered a handful of people who recall visiting Earth from other star systems.[95] But all such contact was in the far past. Apparently souls do not jump back and forth between species."

"You mean 'once a human, always a human'?" I asked.

"Oh no. Just that all of one's lives as a human seem to be grouped together, rather than mixed in with alien existences."

---

[93] Walsch, *Conversations with God,* Book 3, p. 271.

[94] Walsch, *Conversations with God, Book 3*, p. 323.

[95] Newton, Michael, "Early Visitations to Earth by Superior Beings," *Fate,* Vol. 54, No. 3, March 2001, pp. 26-27.

I paused a moment to consume a slice of the bruschetta sitting before us. I was glad we had ordered something that was good at room temperature, as it was difficult to find a moment to eat during our conversations. Washing it down with a swallow of beer, I asked him: "Do you think it's possible that aliens are the sole cause? That all phenomena we now think of as psychic are really a result of advanced technology from other galaxies?"

"Do you recall the ten reasons that reincarnation is not an illusion caused by discarnate spirits?"

I nodded yes.

"Well, most of those reasons make equally strong arguments against the 'illusion-caused-by-aliens' idea. For instance, to accept such a hypothesis would mean believing that each of us has one or more aliens watching over our shoulders, ready at all times to relate consistent stories of past lives, just in case we decide to be hypnotically regressed."

"That is rather inconceivable," I agreed.

"And just as reincarnation is supported by those who speak from the afterlife, so the idea of Survival is supported by the testimony of aliens. If you look up that book on Uri Geller that we mentioned earlier, I believe you'll find a good example of this."

[In this book, the esteemed scientist Andrija Puharich, who was investigating Uri Geller, tells of several communications from entities claiming to be from a far-distant planet. They spoke via a tape recorder and the tapes either were erased afterwards or simply vanished in front of Puharich's eyes. {These same entities claimed that they were the power behind Geller's ability to make objects disappear.} In response to the question "What is the nature of the soul?" they stated: "It inhabits different worlds at different times in its existence. When the physical body dies, it goes with all of its being to its own world. There it carries on with the next phase of its existence. It may go on to other spaces, or it may even return to an earth physical body for another round of existence — what humans call reincarnation may occur."[96]]

Well then," I responded, "what about the other way round? Could UFO's actually be spirits?"

"As in God is my starship's co-pilot?" he asked while motioning for our check.

"Not exactly. If reports from the other side are true, then many souls find themselves in a place where thoughts easily become things. You know, like in that

---

[96] Puharich, Andrija, *Uri: A Journal of the Mystery of Uri Geller*, Bantam Books, 1974, p. 211.

movie where Robin Williams is trying to rescue his wife from her self-imposed hell."

"What Dreams May Come."

"Yeah. So what if someone with a love of science fiction movies dies on this plane and awakens on one like that and decides to create a reality of silvery flying disks. And then, suppose that one of these inter-dimensional bleed-throughs occurs and his creation is seen, for a moment or so, by witnesses in our physical reality. That would explain a lot, wouldn't it?"

"Actually, that could explain a phenomenon that has puzzled UFO researchers – and delighted their critics – for a long time: Strange craft seen in the skies often seem to be one step ahead of current technology. Before hot air balloons were first launched, there were reports of mysterious balloon-shaped objects hovering near the earth. Before airplanes officially flew, bi-planes were witnessed landing on the prairies. And triangular craft were seen in several locations years before stealth bombers were built.

"Perhaps, in some cases at least, these phantoms were the heavenly manifestations of the dreams of those inventors who passed on before their plans were physically constructed. Yep, you could be on to something there."

Rational Witnesses

For awhile, he seemed to be mulling over this idea, but then he took a new tack. "Your agile thinking reminds me of another similarity between reports of psychic phenomena and aerial anomalies, and that is the type of person making the reports. Those who testify to having these strange experiences are generally above average in intelligence, education, and income.[97] And they have a minimal interest in organized religion."

"That sure is contrary to what the überskeptics would have the public believe," I commented.

"Yes, and that false image — a gaggle of ignorant fanatics claiming visitations by Martians or visions of Mary — is too often the one propagated by the media in search of a titillating tale. The very same media," he added, "that blithely ignore the constant stream of research reports and other valid evidence in support of both Survival and UFOs.

With that, we tipped our bartender and made our way to the elevator. We found a fellow conferee awaiting its arrival, so we felt comfortable continuing our discussion as we boarded.

---

[97] Steiger, Brad, "Smart People See Ghosts: Higher Education Supports Belief in the Paranormal," *Fate*, Vol. 59, No. 4, April 2006, pp. 52-56.

"It occurs to me that there is one final characteristic shared by angels and aliens."

"And that would be?"

"That would be that they have both been visiting earth since ancient times."

"Ahh," I said, "you must be referring to the clay tablets that tell of beings from space arriving in Sumer some 6,000 years ago."

"Those are the oldest writings we know of — at least so far — and they tell a remarkable tale of strange beings, spaceships, and genetic engineering. But they're not the only examples. The Judeo-Christian Bible contains several reports of seemingly physical beings coming down from the skies and interacting with humans. And such stories can be found in the folklore of almost every culture around the world."

"I've always thought of such stories as merely myths."

"Easy enough to so dismiss one or two," he replied as we stepped out of the elevator, "but when you learn how widespread and similar they are, you realize that there must be some truth behind the tales."

"So," I attempted to summarize, "the spirits claim that ETs are real, and the aliens believe in souls, yet the earthly manifestations of both are almost the same. That's more than a bit puzzling."

"The same in many ways and yet different in some. Tell me," he asked, stopping my stroll with a hand on my arm, "what do you hear?"

I listened for a moment. Only one other person was walking down the corridor ahead of us. Then the guy turned and entered a room. "Just that fellow's foot-steps and the door closing," I answered.

"Well, according to the reports I've read, if that figure was not a human, then he was likely a spir-it, not a space brother. The sound of footsteps is virtually always a ghostly phenomenon."

Listening to our own footfalls as we resumed walking, I thought about various alien-sighting, encounter, and abduction reports I had heard or read. UFOs are almost always reported as moving soundlessly, even when performing high speed aerobatics right over the ob-servers' heads. Greys and other beings seem to glide silently over the ground and never speak aloud. I real-ized that sound of any sort was uncannily rare in all UFO reports.

Then, another thought occurred to me. "But ghosts and spirits are likely two different phenomena. I know that poltergeists are noisy but aren't most spirits just as quiet as aliens?"

"Tell that to the Fox family," he said.

As discussed at the beginning of this book, the Fox family gained fame in 1848 when a spirit began communicating with them via loud rapping sounds.

"You're right. I never heard of aliens rapping … although," I grinned at him, "some rappers do seem pretty alien to me."

He rolled his eyes at that, but he couldn't totally suppress a smile. We had reached his room and he swiped his keycard in the lock. "When you're ready for breakfast, come and *rap* on my door," he said, his grin getting wider.

At a loss for a witty repartee, I just grinned back and headed on down to my room.

Note: An excellent source of information on UFOs is the website: http://www.paradigmresearchgroup.org/

A few of the better books on the subject are: *Above Top Secret* by Timothy Good; *Clear Intent* by Lawrence Fawcett; and *Confrontations* by Jacques Vallee.

Charles Richet

A physiologist, chemist, bacteriologist, pathologist, psychologist, and aviation pioneer, Richet received his doctorate in medicine in 1869 and in science in 1878. He served as professor of physiology at the medical school of the University of Paris for 38 years.

Richet was awarded the Nobel Prize for his research on anaphylaxis, he contributed much to research on the nervous system, anesthesia, serum therapy, and neuro-muscular stimuli. He served as editor of the Revue Scientifique for 24 years and contributed to many other scientific publications.

In His Own Words:

"The idolatry of current ideas was so dominant at that time that no pains were taken either to verify or to refute Crookes' statements. Men were content to ridicule them, and I avow with shame that I was among the willfully blind. Instead of admiring the heroism of a recognized man of science who dared then in 1872 to say that there really are phantoms that can be photographed and whose heartbeats can be heard, I laughed."[98]

---

[98] Richet, Charles, *Thirty Years of Psychical Research*, W. Collins Sons & Co., Ltd., 1923, p. 31.

"To ask a physiologist, a physicist, or a chemist to admit that a form that has a circulation of blood, warmth, and muscles, that exhales carbonic acid, has weight, speaks, and thinks, can issue from a human body is to ask of him an intellectual effort that is really painful.

"Yes, it is absurd, but no matter – it is true."[99]

---

[99] *Ibid.*, p. 544.

Memories of Home

Near-death experiences may suggest an afterlife, but other lines of evidence more directly prove false the arguments against survival. These lines include the evidence for reincarnation.

– Chris Carter[100]

Family Lost & Found
[Case ID# 61, ESS Score = 270, Current Rank 16th]

'Tis an oft-told tale, both sad and inspiring: a woman driven by guilt and worry strives to locate the family she was forced to abandon years before. There's a most uncommon twist to the tale Jenny Cockell tells, however, for when she finally finds her lost children, they are all several decades older than their mother.

From a very young age, Jenny Cockell (pronounced ki-KELL) was plagued by unexplained dreams and visions in which she was a woman named Mary. She seemed to be reliving Mary's life or, more often, re-dying Mary's death. Night after night, Jenny's dreams were filled with the panic of a 30-something

---

[100] Carter, Chris, *Science and the Near-Death Experience: How Consciousness Survives Death*, Inner Traditions, 2010.

woman lying in a hospital bed, racked with pain yet suffering even more from the thought of dying and forsaking her children. During the day, Cockell's visions were of more pleasant times with the woman's numerous children – she could envision at least seven of them, but she felt that there may have been more.

In addition to Mary's children and her final hours, the young Cockell had visions (which seemed like memories to her) of a home and village that, although she had never traveled outside England, she somehow knew were located in Ireland. As a child, she often drew maps of this village and described her home as a two-room cottage, sitting first on the left of a country lane and turned sideways to it. She envisioned where the cottage's windows were and what pictures hung on the interior walls. She felt that Mary had two older brothers who had gone away from the area. Altogether, Jenny Cockell had memories involving scores of minutia about a place far away and a life that ended some 21 years before she was born.

At school, Cockell studied a map of Ireland and felt drawn to the town of Malahide about 10 miles north of Dublin. She longed to travel there and confirm her visions, but it was not until she was 33 years of age and a married mother with two children of her own that she managed to get the money, the time, and the confidence to make the trip. Once she discovered that her inner-knowledge of the town did actually match quite well with current reality, Cockell was emboldened to begin a determined quest to locate and contact Mary's children.

She scoured libraries, spoke with priests, wrote letters to historical societies and orphanages, placed newspaper ads, underwent hypnosis, and even made calls to names found in Ireland's phone books. Her search went into high gear when she located a man who had lived in Malahide as a youth. He had gone to school, he said, with some children whose mother's name was Mary and who had lived with a large number of siblings in a two-room cottage that sat sideways, first on the left from the start of Swords lane. The family's last name, he said, was Sutton. This surname, which Cockell had never been able to recall, was the key that enabled her to locate, contact, meet, and ultimately befriend five of Mary's children.

The story of Cockell's search and the discovery of innumerable bits of confirming evidence is well told in her book. Also, she has appeared, either alone or with Mary's 60- and 70-something children, on several televised programs including, in the U.S., *20/20 with Barbara Walters, Donahue, Sightings* and *The Unexplained*.

As far as the evidence is concerned, the maps Cockell drew as a child are virtually the same as those anyone might hand-draw of the same roads today. Likewise, the largest church in the town could easily be picked out by anyone who had seen her sketches. Cockell's descriptions of her childhood dreams and drawings have been publicly backed up by testimony from her mother.[101] And then, we have the downright amazing fact that several siblings have testified that Jenny Cockell demonstrated to them a knowledge of their early home life so intimate and detailed that they are convinced that she incarnates the spirit of their long-dead mother. This despite their lifetime immersion in a religious doctrine that denies any such possibility.

Today, a search on the Net for "Jenny Cockell" will get many thousands of hits, including a few informative videos. Also, of course, there are skeptical commentaries claiming to explain or expose the case, but I have found none of these to be either factual or objective. Just to take one example, an article in the *Skeptical Inquirer* says, in part:

> "She turned then to actual research, publishing an ad in a Mensa magazine, sending out numerous form letters, acquiring maps, and so on. Eventually she turned up a village (Malahide), a road (Swords Road), and finally a woman named Mary Sutton who roughly fit the target. ... Unfortunately, Cockell's intriguing and no doubt sincere saga does not withstand critical analysis. First, consider the overwhelming lack of factual information provided by the dreams and hypnosis. Unknown were Mary's surname, either maiden or married,

---

[101] A&E *Sightings* on reincarnation, available on DVD from A&E.com.

or the names of her husband or children. Similarly, the village's name and even its location were a mystery."[102]

Apparently, this critic had not taken the trouble to actually read the book he is denigrating, for it clearly states that Cockell, while still a young girl, had selected the town of Malahide using a map of Ireland in her school atlas. A map that was far too small of scale to allow any matching with the sketches she had made. So, the village was not "turned up" as part of her adult research and neither its name nor its location "were a mystery." Furthermore, while it is true that every name could not be recalled, this critic manages to avoid mentioning the many "unknowable" details that Cockell *did* know about the children and the events in the family's life. The eldest boy was in his seventies when he stated on record that she knew things about his childhood that even his brothers and sisters did not know.

As for possible alternative explanations, clairvoyance and cosmic databases clearly have no parts to play. Although all of the confirmed information did exist in one mind or another, the idea of super-duper mental telepathy is negated: first, because there was no earthly link between Cockell and any of those minds, and second, because the children had been separated at

---

[102] "A Case of Reincarnation — Reexamined," by Joe Nickell, *Skeptical Inquirer*, Vol. 8.1, March 1998.

their mother's death and had little or no contact since – the youngest did not even know she had siblings.

The Rebirth of Bridey Murphy
[Case ID# 36, ESS Score = 274, Current Rank 12th]

The phrase "a household name" has rarely been more truly applied than it was to the name Bridey Murphy during the late 1950s and early '60s. The impact of Morey Bernstein's book, *The Search for Bridey Murphy*, was felt in virtually every city, town, and hamlet in the Western world because it suggested that the theretofore alien concept of reincarnation was a demonstrable fact. In the media frenzy that followed the book's release – it was even made into a movie – numerous falsehoods were circulated as debunkers and überskeptics attempted to undermine the evidence. These days, the idea of reincarnation is not so novel and the brouhaha over Bernstein's book seems almost a bit of quaint Americana; nevertheless, the evidence remains strong and the tale fascinating.

Only a brief summary of that tale can be told here. For the full story, read the 1965 version of Bernstein's engrossing book. This is referred to as "the counterattack version" as it includes full rebuttals to all the misinformation spread by overzealous critics. Also, Bernstein had LP records made from the session tapes and some may still be available via the Internet.

Before looking into who was Bridey Murphy, it is important to know who was Morey Bernstein. Some detractors like to picture the man as a dabbler in occult arts and/or an opportunistic seeker of fortune and fame. In fact, Bernstein was a well-to-do and highly respected businessman in both New York and Colorado, where he served on the board of directors of four leading firms. Bernstein was a pragmatic man who had once walked out on a stage demonstration of hypnotism because he wanted to make certain that his friends knew that "this silly business" was beneath his intelligence. Not until years later, when he witnessed a demonstration in a friend's home, did he decide that hypnotism was a subject worth pursuing. Over a period of 10 years, he became highly skilled at his new avocation. Often the local medical community would request his services to hypnotize a patient and he always complied without accepting any compensation. Furthermore, he did not seek publicity. When a friend of his suggested that a newspaper reporter write an article about his experiences, he was quite resistant to the idea.

Why Bernstein, a materialistic scoffer who laughed at hypnotism and was repulsed by the concept of reincarnation, came to champion both, is a story well told in his book. Suffice it to say that on his very first attempt to regress someone back beyond her infancy, his patient, Virginia Tighe, recalled several previous lives — one of which was as an Irish girl named Bridget Kathleen Murphy who referred to herself as "Bridey." In that session, and five more ensuing, she provided a richly detailed description of her life during the first half of the 19th century. Hundreds of facts were given that were most unlikely to be known by Tighe.[103] More than a few of these were thought wrong by scholars but were proved correct through diligent research.

Particularly striking examples of "impossible-to-know" facts are Bridey's statements that, while living in Belfast, she brought "foodstuffs" at "John Carrigan's" and at "Farr's." No one living in Belfast, or anywhere else, could confirm that such establishments ever existed, until a local librarian, after weeks of searching, found a directory for 1865 that listed both as greengrocers doing business in the same sector of the city. The two grocer's names were given during different sessions and, by themselves, constitute powerful evidence that Bridey's story is exactly what it claims to be.

Another convincing piece is Bridey's statement that, in her youth in Cork, she lived "outside the village" in a place called "The Meadows" where she had no neighbors. Again, the "Meadows" was unheard of at the time of the regressions, but researchers later

---

[103] In an attempt to protect her privacy, Bernstein calls his subject "Ruth Simmons," but her actual name was soon made public. Virginia Tighe had to be cajoled to participate in the sessions as neither she nor her husband had any interest in pursuing past lives, and they both shunned the public eye.

found an 1801 map of the Cork area that shows a large pastoral area called "Mardike Meadows" just to the west of the city. This is the only "meadows" on the map. No more than eight buildings are shown, spread throughout 82 acres of land. Thus the area perfectly fits Bridey's description in location, population, and name.

No one, living or dead, could reasonably be expected to recite hundreds of details about their life and never make a mistake, but, so far, none of Bridey's statements have been proved false and no contradictions discovered. Time and again, the "experts" have claimed that Bridey was wrong about one arcane point or another, only to see her vindicated by further research. Her use of the term "slip" to mean a child's frock, or "linen" instead of handkerchief, are just two of many such instances. According to William J. Barker, a journalist who spent weeks in Ireland investigating various statements: "Bridey was dead right on at least two dozen facts 'Ruth' (Virginia Tighe) could not have acquired in [America], even if she had set out deliberately to study up on Irish obscurities."

As for the possibility of there being other information sources in Tighe's life, despite the fanciful inventions of those desperate to undermine her story, the fact is that no source other than a past-life memory is either feasible or credible.

The Strangers Were Lovers
[Case ID# 60, ESS Score = 274, Current Rank 11th]

As far as I can tell, this case is unique in reincarnation literature. Most cases involve one hypnotherapist and one subject who recalls one or more past lives. Sometimes there is solid evidence to precisely confirm the recalled events; often the evidence is merely supportive or suggestive. The evidential basis for a very few cases comes from the agreement of two or more subjects recalling participation in the same past-life event while being separately regressed by the same hypnotherapist. The case discussed here goes a step beyond the others in that it involves two different subjects recalling the same lives while being regressed by two different therapists in sessions that were both many miles and several years apart.

Entirely unknown to one another, a woman in Georgia in 1984 and a man in Florida in 1989 recalled associated lifetimes in Ohio in the early 1900s. During a unique joint session, their love affair and tragic deaths were recounted by both, to the amazement of several witnesses. There could be many similar occurrences, but most will never be known due to the privacy typically observed by therapists and patients. The exceptional nature of this case only came to light because Jack Turnock happened to be watching a rerun of *Unsolved Mysteries* in which a woman named Georgia Rudolph was recalling a past life. Her name in that life, she remembered was Sandra Jean Jenkins and she had a boyfriend named Tommy Hicks. As he watched the show, Turnock says, he began to have strange feelings. When the name Hicks was mentioned, he reports, "Even though I knew what she was going to say, it still felt like I was punched in the solar plexus."

Turnock, now a university professor, had undergone hypnotic regression at his wife's request because she was considering giving a session to her mother as a birthday present. During his session — with Dr. Bruce Crystal in Jacksonville, Florida — Turnock found himself re-living scenes from the life of a boy in Ohio around the turn of the last century, a boy named Tom Hicks.

Since early childhood, Georgia Rudolph had been haunted by unexplained memories and recurring dreams in which she seemed to be a young girl – some of the times the girl was about 8 years of age, other times about 18 – living an upper-middle-class life around the turn of the century. She could picture the girl vividly and used to spend hours with her crayons trying to capture her face. The memories were often so realistic that she could feel the icy cold air as she seemed to ride in an open carriage, could smell the horses and the leather of their harnesses, could hear their hoofs striking the pavement.

As she knew that she had been adopted at the age of 5, Rudolph at first assumed that these images must be associated with her earliest childhood. When she queried her birth relatives, however, they could recall no correspondent experiences.

At the age of 33, determined to uncover the cause of her dreams and memories that had troubled her so long, Rudolph consulted Dr. Douglas Smith, a clinical psychologist who was the deputy director of a mental health center in Macon, Georgia. At the time, Rudolph did not believe in reincarnation. In fact, she says that the idea frightened her because it "went against everything that I have ever been taught as far as religion goes." Smith wasn't expecting a past-life recall either. He states that, when he began to treat Rudolph, "reincarnation was probably the last thing in my mind about what had happened to her."

During the initial session, after Smith had regressed her to the approximate age of 2, she suddenly stopped responding. When he persisted in calling her name, she said "I don't know who you're talking too." So Smith said, "Well, if you aren't Georgia, who are you?" And she responded, "My name is Sandra Jean Jenkins."

Throughout this and subsequent sessions, "Jenkins" provided an abundance of information about her life as a girl who was born in 1895 and raised in or near a small city beside a river. Although she never specifically identified the town, the name "Marietta" kept surfacing and she deduced that Marietta, Ohio was the location of the recalled events. When the sessions were concluded, Dr. Smith testified: "Georgia seems to me a very down-to-earth person ... I think that she's a very stable individual ... She is not faking or pretending." As further testament to her character, the producers of the television segment stated, "What's definite about Georgia's story is that, meeting her and spending the time we spent with her while we were doing this story, you know she wasn't making this up."[104]

Rudolph's memories of special significance include:

- Many scenes on a stern-wheel riverboat, and a feeling that it belonged to her family.
- Her fiancé named Tommy Hicks by whom she was pregnant.
- Tommy's parents were named Tom and Jennie Hicks.
- Walking from a church through a graveyard to a specific tombstone. She could not read the name on the stone, but she saw that it was near the statue of an angel with one arm upraised.
- A large white house that felt like home.
- The death of Hicks just prior to their wedding when his boat hit a sandbar in a storm and he was swept from the deck.
- Her grief at his death and her shame over her pregnancy leading her to suicide by drowning.

In 1985, Rudolph traveled the 640 miles to Marietta, Ohio. While touring Marietta with Ted Bauer (a life-

---

[104] Quoted from commentaries by John Cosgrove and Raymond Bridgers on the *Unsolved Mysteries: Psychics* compilation DVD.

time resident who was the retired City Editor of the local newspaper) Rudolph demonstrated an intimate familiarity with the town. Whatever Bauer couldn't confirm from personal knowledge he researched and he uncovered no inaccuracies in Rudolph's descriptions. The television production featured a scene in which Rudolph stopped in front of an insurance office and described an ice-cream parlor that used to be in that location. Bauer stated, "She described the interior [as it was when Jenkins lived] almost perfectly. I checked this with the son of the man who had run it for years." That interior had been re-done in 1937.

Driving 5 miles north to Newport, Ohio, Rudolph found a house that felt very much like the one in her dreams. Around the turn of the century, the house had been owned by a family named Greene. These same Greenes owned a fleet of stern-wheelers.[105] Then she found the church that she had so often seen while asleep. When she walked the path – so familiar from her dreams – twixt the church and the grave, Rudolph found that the surname on the tombstone was Greene. And, yes, clearly visible nearby was the statue of an angel with one arm pointing heavenward.

---

[105] A photograph of the sternwheeler from which Tommy Hicks is thought to have fallen is viewable in the case file at www.SurvivalTop40.com.

Altogether, a most evidential case that argues strongly for the reality of reincarnation, even without considering the factor that makes it so special.

The apparent link between his own past-life recollections and those of Georgia Rudolph stunned and perplexed Turnock. "I didn't know what to do with the information," he says, so he "decided to deal with it by not dealing with it." And so, six months passed until one day he happened to turn on his television only to be confronted by yet another re-run of the disturbing *Unsolved Mysteries* segment. Once again, Turnock was both fascinated and agitated by the show. This time, his wife decided to do something about this disruption to her household, so she wrote a letter to Dr. Smith describing the situation. Smith contacted the show's producers who ultimately decided that Turnock was for real and that a follow-up show should be made in which Rudolph and Turnock would be videotaped during a joint hypnosis session.

The filming (or rather, the attempted filming) was done in Smith's office in Macon, Georgia. Turnock was not allowed to meet Rudolph until after he was regressed. During his regression, Turnock (as Hicks) recalled many details about his life and death on a riverboat named the N.B. Forrest. Afterwards, Rudolph asked him where Hicks had proposed to Jenkins and where they were when she had gotten pregnant. Turnock replied that the proposal took place on a bench by the river. As for the conception: "You walk from Gordon Green's house away from town on the road by the river. When you get to a corn field turn right. There's a small bluff overlooking the river where they used to go. That day they had a picnic in the corner of the field and that's where they made love and Sandra Jean got pregnant." According to Turnock, "Rudolf's jaw nearly hit the floor. What I described was exactly what she had seen in her hypnosis sessions."

In the afternoon, Dr. Smith hypnotized both Rudolph and Turnock together. Turnock describes the experience as being the weirdest part of all. "We both went under fairly easily and we began talking to each other as Tom and Sandra Jean. It was the most surreal experience of my life. It was as if another person had taken over my body and I was watching it happen. Tom told Sandra Jean how he was sorry he left her that way. She forgave him. They/we held hands, reiterated our love and said goodbye. It was incredibly emotional. I was so drained I couldn't move for half an hour. Jim Lindsey, the *Unsolved Mysteries* director was literally dancing around, saying it was the best sequence they ever filmed."

Trouble was, they did not actually film the session. Although the equipment was turned on, the cables were connected, and the scene was showing on the monitor, the videotape recorded nothing but static. How and why this bewildering failure occurred is perhaps the biggest unsolved mystery of all.

No written record of a Sandra Jean Jenkins has been found in Marietta or Newport, Ohio, but there is a record of a Tom and Jennie Hicks (who could well have been Tommy's parents) buying a farm in Newport in 1906. Rudolph thinks that no records were kept of Jenkins because the girl committed suicide. Perhaps that is correct, or perhaps the records were accidently destroyed, or perhaps they will be uncovered yet. It is also conceivable that the name "Sandra Jean Jenkins" is some sort of spiritual pseudonym intended to protect the reputation of the Greene family. Whatever the case, the evidentiality of the case must rest on something other than public records.

Those skeptics who rely on some imagined form of super-ESP to explain what they cannot otherwise understand, should consider the lack of links between the house, the boats, and the grave. Since Rudolph had not been able to discern the Greene name in her dreams, neither telepathy nor clairvoyance could have associated the grave site with the house – or the river boats with either. Her inability to read the stone, therefore, strengthens the case considerably.

The most convincing aspect of Rudolph's recall is her intimate knowledge of Marietta, Ohio. On first considering the evidence, Rudolph's description of the pre-renovation interior of the ice-cream parlor seems the highlight of the tour. One cannot rule out, however, that she was simply lucky that her idea of a turn-of-the-century parlor (perhaps gleaned from an old movie) just happened to match reality. Of course, that doesn't explain how she knew that there ever *was* an ice-cream parlor at that location, or how she knew so many other minor details about an unsung little city she had never visited. Even her tour guide, a tough old reporter whom the TV producers called "as skeptical a person as you will ever see,"[106] admitted that he was baffled because she knew more about the place than most lifelong residents.

As for the joint regression session, the unrecorded tape will, no doubt, provide fodder for the skeptics who will view the missing video as suspicious; perhaps even attempting to dismiss the entire case because one part of it was not recorded. I suspect, however, that if the videotape had recorded perfectly, these same skeptics would simply claim (or, at least, imply) that the whole session had been faked for television. The important validation is the number of participants and crew who either have corroborated or have never contradicted the facts presented here.

The evidence from Rudolph's regressions is impressive in its own right; the agreement between Rudolph and Turnock on the details of the marriage proposal and the love-making between Jenkins and Hicks

---

[106] Quoted from commentaries by John Cosgrove and Raymond Bridgers on the *Unsolved Mysteries: Psychics* compilation DVD.

makes this case truly exceptional and exceptionally convincing.

Sources
Memories of Home

Family Lost and Found
Cockell, Jenny, *Across Time and Death*, Simon & Schuster, 1993.
The television program segments mentioned first aired on ABC in 1994, on CBS and NBC in 1995, and on A&E in 1998 respectively. Cockell's story was also the inspiration for a made-for-TV movie titled *Yesterday's Children*, which was first broadcast in October 2000.

The Rebirth of Bridey Murphy
Bernstein, Morey, *The Search for Bridey Murphy*, Lancer Books, Inc., 1965.

The Strangers Were Lovers
Unsolved Mysteries, season 2, episode 21, first airing on 14 February 1990.
Details of Turnock's involvement are taken largely from a written statement he submitted to the author on 17 February 2010. Miscellaneous facts were gleaned from telephone interviews with Rudolph and with Turnock.

Chapter Fourteen

An "Eary" Dinner

Souls don't return promiscuously to any body, in any family. There is a sequence in their lives that necessitates their coming to one particular environment. It is part of the natural law, and works automatically.[107]

We were tucked in a corner of the hotel dining room under a picture of President Lincoln and his son that hung above the mantle of a large fireplace. Our two dinner companions had been discussing the old man's presentation on various reincarnation cases when Jenny Cockell's search for her elderly children was mentioned. I took this opportunity to bring up a related subject. "Although I accept the Cockell case as providing convincing evidence for Survival and reincarnation, there is one aspect of it that bothers me."

"What's so special about that case?"

"Not really special. In fact, it's something that pops up a lot in reincarnation cases — it's the claim that the person today physically resembles the person they re-

---

[107] Kelway-Bamber, L., *Claude's Book*, 1919, p. 31.

call being in a past life. On the Donahue show, Mary's 75-year-old son made a big deal of how Jenny has the same eyes as his mother has in an old photograph. I just don't get it. People look like their parents or their grand-parents, or maybe the milk man or the …"

"You're really showing your age there; it's been many decades since anyone delivered milk to my stoop."

"Actually, dairy deliveries have been making a bit of a comeback lately. But whether the milkman, the post-man, the pool boy, or whomever, it's DNA that deter-mines how we look. Are we to believe that genetics can be overruled by the spirits of lives past?"

"I sympathize with your skepticism," he said, as a waitress distributed menus around our table, "and I cannot endorse such a connection, but there is a rather fascinating story that argues for it."

"We're all ears," I said, glancing around the table for confirmation.

"How apropos," he grinned, "for in my punnier moments I think of this as an 'ear-ry' tale.[108]

---

[108] This case was first published in *La Revue Métapsychique* in 1948 by Dr. Maurice Delarrey. For further information in English, see Ian Stevenson's book *European Cases of the Reincarnation Type*, pages 42 - 44.

"In the early part of the 20th Century, in a small village in France, a man and his wife enjoyed passing many evenings by experimenting with a talking board. The wife — let's call her 'Marie' — sat at the table in a sort of trance, her fingers lightly touching the planchette as it moved, seemingly of its own volition from letter to letter. Meanwhile her husband — 'Pierre' — would ask questions and take note of the answers as they were spelled out."

"A most typical arrangement," I observed, peeking at the menu and hoping that this tale would not much delay the satisfaction of my growing hunger.

"Yes; women are generally more adept at tuning in to the spirit plane. But the spirit communication that makes this case atypical occurred one evening in 1924 when a name was spelled out that the husband did not recognize. After some consideration, the wife recalled that her father had once had a servant by that name, a servant whose right ear stuck out in a most conspicuous way. During an ensuing session, the spirit returned and acknowledged that he had served as a servant to that family and he announced that he was preparing to return to the same.

"Pierre was intrigued by this revelation and quizzed the spirit further. It seems that the spirit had selected a relative of theirs who lived in a distant town and already had two daughters. This time, the spirit said, they would have a son and he provided the exact date of the birth to come – some four months in the future.

" 'All very well,' said Pierre, who was unaware that his relative was pregnant, 'but how shall we know that the boy is you? After all, you might just be good at predicting the future.' "

"Don't tell me," I interjected. "Let me guess … by his ear!"

"Ahh, such an intelligent lad you are," he observed in a tone that suggested a matronly pat on the head. "Yes, the spirit replied that Marie would easily recognize the babe by its ear."

"And, would my exceptional intellect be correct in predicting that ensuing events proved the spirit correct?"

"It would indeed. On the morning specified, a son was born to the named family. But it was not until three months later that Pierre and Marie were invited to a family reunion at the new infant's household. Upon arrival, the couple were at once escorted into the nursery by the new mother who warned them that the child was in an unusual mood, breaking out into tears every time she brought someone new to the side of the crib.

"Well, as you have likely guessed, when Marie approached, the babe began to smile and stretched out his hands toward her. The mother actually exclaimed 'Look at that! One might have thought he knew you.'"

With that, the old man opened his menu and stared down at it.

I played along, took a drink of my iced tea, waited several seconds, and then coughed and said, "Uh … the ear?"

"Oh yes, the ear." He peered over the menu for a moment, eyes twinkling, and then continued. "Well, there was a bandage over the infant's right ear. When Pierre asked about it — trying to sound as if he knew nothing — the mother replied that it wasn't anything to be concerned about; that the fetus must have developed in a 'bad position' in her womb, causing his ear to stick out from his head. The doctor had assured her that the ear would look perfectly normal in a few months.

"Whether or not it did, was not revealed by the researcher who reported the case."

"Fascinating," I remarked. "That suggests the possibility that birthmarks corresponding to wounds and injuries are imprinted on the babe intentionally rather than being a natural consequence of the re-birth process."

"Now that is a wide-open field for research. As you know, Stevenson published a two-volume set on the links between biology and reincarnation, although I don't recall the good doctor consulting any spirits as to what the intent is behind these appearances."

"Well," I said, setting down my menu as I saw the waitress approaching with pad in hand, "Stevenson faced derision enough from mainstream science for even bothering to investigate such occurrences. It's too bad, really, that researchers don't try more often to hypnotically regress people who have spontaneous recall of a past life to see if their waking memories are matched by their entranced ones.

"I believe I'll have the Chicken Chesapeake …"

Julian Ochorowicz

Professor of psychology and philosophy at the University of Warsaw, Ochorowicz was the leader of the Positivist movement in Poland, and one of the founders of the Polish Psychological Institute.

He received his doctorate from Leipzig University and became assistant professor at Lwów University in 1881, subsequently spent several years in Paris, where he was co-director of the Institut General Psychologique.

In His Own Words:

"I found I had done a great wrong to men who had proclaimed new truths at the risk of their positions. When I remember that I branded as a fool that fearless investigator, Crookes, the inventor of the radiometer, because he had the courage to assert the reality of psychic phenomena and to subject them to scientific tests, and when I also recollect that I used to read his articles thereon in the same stupid style, regarding him as crazy, I am ashamed, both of myself and others, and I cry from the very bottom of my heart. 'Father, I have sinned against the Light.'"[109]

---

[109] Tweedale, Charles, *Man's Survival After Death*, The Psychic Book Club, 1925, p. 470.

Memories of War

How soon does an entity reincarnate? This is not a set pattern or rule. It is dependent on the free will of that particular entity. Also upon the needs of that entity. If it is one that has been greatly damaged or hurt in one particular incarnation ... it is then incarnated rather quickly. [110]

Of the thousands of past lives that entranced subjects have recalled, only a few have provided evidential statements that can be corroborated. This is mostly because the average time between lives is so long that any specific information recalled is historically obscure, if available at all. Today's better record-keeping bodes well for a higher rate of confirmation in the future. This may not increase the rate of acceptance, however, since better records mean easier access by non-psychic means.

One factor that can shorten the time spent between earthly visits is sudden, violent death, such as so-often occurs in wartime. This means that the detailed records

---

[110] Boulton, Peter, *Psychic Beam to Beyond,* 1983, p. 71.

kept by military organizations in the 20th century can be examined to corroborate the recollections of past lives as soldiers and sailors. The following are three of the best examples of such confirmed recalls.

Round Trip to Allentown
[Case ID# 63, ESS Score = 267, Current Rank 20th]

Unlike the typical subject of hypnotic age regression who seeks relief from symptoms unexplained in their current life, Tim Stewart sought only to write an article for a national magazine. A computer programmer and freelance journalist, Stewart was living in Albuquerque, New Mexico, when he was given the assignment to write about past-life therapy. To research the subject — about which he was more than dubious — he underwent several hypnotic regressions.

During his fourth session, Stewart experienced being a soldier, and seemed to be reliving battles somewhere in North Africa during the second world war. Now, it is not unusual for hypnotized subjects to recall emotional scenes of fighting and dying, but Stewart went way beyond such general descriptions. He not only gave the soldier's name — William Max— but named his army unit — the 47th Infantry, 9th Division — and gave his blood type, his date of death, and his army ID number. Furthermore, Stewart recalled that Max was born on May 27, 1919 and had grown up in Allentown, Pennsylvania.

And so, as any good journalist would, Stewart called the main library in Allentown and inquired as to the existence of a previous resident named William Max. One month later, Stewart received a copy of an obituary from the local Allentown newspaper dated April 11, 1943. It read, in part, "Fun-loving Bill Max, popular basketball player on the Jewish Community Center team and the 6th Ward Democratic Club team, went down fighting in defense of his country. ... The official War Department message sent to his father, Jacob Max, read: 'The Secretary of War desires that I tender his deep sympathy to you in the loss of your son Private William Max.' "

These facts and others confirmed in the obituary encouraged Stewart to make inquiries of the Department of Defense. Yes he was told, the identification number Stewart had seen on Max's dog tags while entranced did, indeed, belong to an army Private named William Max, who was killed while fighting in North Africa, in 1943.

This story presents strong evidence for Survival, but there is an epilogue that might make it even more convincing to those doubters who would grasp at the straw of super-ESP and claim that Stewart got all the information by clairvoyantly accessing old newspaper clippings and military archives. In 1993, Stewart returned to Pennsylvania — a place he had not been since he was a toddler — to attend the funeral of his favorite uncle. While at the funeral, Stewart encountered an elderly woman who was a stranger to him, yet she insisted that he looked familiar to her. In response to her queries, he told her his name and the names of various relatives, but she could not make the connection she sought. Then Stewart asked her name and she replied, "Thelma Max."

Further conversations revealed that Thelma Max was the widow of the brother of William Max. Once she made the connection, she realized that it was her deceased brother-in-law she was reminded of when she looked into Stewart's eyes. Stewart and Max do have similar features, but an outsider would never think they were the same man.

Because of this "chance" encounter, Stewart met other members of the Max family, visited his childhood home, and wandered the neighborhood where William had grown up. Harold Schentzle, a boyhood friend of William Max heard about Stewart's incredible story and arranged a meeting. Schentzle had serious doubts about Stewart's claims and he thought he had the perfect way to settle the matter. After admitting that there was some resemblance, Schentzle asked Stewart if he could recall the last thing that Max said to him prior to embarking for the war. In reply, Stewart told Schentzle that Max had said, "In 1940, I had a dream that if I went into the service and I got shipped overseas, I would never make it home. I'd be killed." Schentzle, who was convinced that Max had never told that dream to anyone but him, fell back in his chair as the blood drained from his face. "To be honest with you," Schentzle reported, "I got goose pimples."

In the ensuing years, most of the Max family has come to accept Stewart as one of them.

A Submariner Resurfaces
[Case ID# 59, ESS Score = 281, Current Rank 3rd]

Some phobias can be fairly simple to live with. Many folks have a fear of spiders, for instance, and manage to get by well enough. A fear of enclosed spaces, on the other hand, is a true handicap in this modern age of elevators and airplanes. Likewise, a fear of water can be most inconvenient when one wants to join friends at the beach … or needs a bath. According to a recent article,[111] claustrophobia and aquaphobia (a.k.a. hydrophobia) are two of the six most commonly experienced phobias. Woe unto the poor soul who suffers from both of these simultaneously.

Bruce Kelly, of Glendora, California, was just such a soul in November of 1987, when he showed up at the office of hypnotherapist Rick Brown. Kelly disclosed that, whenever he was on an airplane, he was overwhelmed with terror the moment the cabin doors were latched. He could think of no reason for this fear. Nor could he explain why he was so very, very afraid of water. He could only shower if his back was to the spray and he was simply unable to force himself to

---

[111] *The Ten Most Common Phobias* on phobias-help.com.

climb into a bathtub. On the few occasions when he had been immersed in water he had become dizzy, nauseous, and suffered from trembling and cramps. On top of all that, he was regularly troubled by stabbing pains in his stomach and chest that no doctor had been able to explain.

Rick Brown was a Certified Hypnotherapist who had successfully treated many patients complaining of inexplicable maladies. Although only about one percent of his patients experienced past-life recall while regressed, he felt that Kelly could well be reacting to events that had occurred in a previous lifetime. Brown hypnotized Kelly and asked him "to recall the time and place where he was first affected by the terror."

The entranced Kelly responded, "I'm in a submarine … I'm dying."

His name, he said, was James Edward Johnston. Then he told a fearsome story of death by drowning in a small, lightless, metal chamber, on the 11th of February, 1942. He said his submarine, the Shark, SS-174, was submerged near Celebes Island when it was attacked by depth-charges for the second time in two days. This time, he was not on duty because he had been confined to his bunk with two broken ribs suffered during the first attack. This time, the Japanese were more accurate, and Johnston was caught in a rush of seawater as he tried to reach his station. He and all the crew were dead before the submarine had settled on the ocean floor.

These specific details and more were revealed during Kelly's first past-life regression. Not only were all of them confirmed by extensive research,[112] the session was successfully therapeutic — his fears of closed spaces and water faded away and he no longer experienced the pains in his torso (apparently caused by his past-life rib injuries).

Despite the goal of the hypnotherapy having been achieved, the therapist was intrigued by the case and wanted to see what else might surface. Although he was a born-again Christian at the time, and could not accept the idea of reincarnation, the subject was likewise curious and agreed to further sessions.

These sessions filled out the life of James Johnston with confirmable facts in a way rarely accomplished before or since. Brown was able to confirm the Johnston-personality's description of the battle theater that included such facts as the names or numbers of four other U.S. subs nearby, their base of operations, the mission of the Shark, and the full names of two other crewman who went down with him.

---

[112] Prior to the Internet, Brown was required to spend many hours searching in libraries, the U.S. Navy Historical Center and Operational Archives, and the Military Reference and Service Branches of the National Archives, in Washington, DC. Of course, the precise whereabouts of Johnston when he died could not be confirmed, as the submarine was not salvaged.

That's hardly the end of the story, however. In trance, Kelly/Johnston described much of his youth and the events that led up to his enlisting in the Navy. He spoke of his joining the Civilian Conservation Corps and being sent to Tule Lake in California, and Scottsboro and Guntersville in Alabama.

Born in Jacksonville, Alabama on February 1, 1921, [All dates and places were confirmed.] he was raised, he claimed, by his unwed mother in one rented bedroom of a company-owned house in the Profile Cotton Mill Village. His mother died young in March of 1936, he said, and he recalled a cousin named Elizabeth in Alabama and a girlfriend named Molly Lassiter, in California. Also, he remembered being especially fond of eating the ends of bread loaves, just as Kelly is currently.

Rick Brown made three trips to Alabama researching the case; on the third, he was accompanied by Bruce Kelly. This trip was filmed, and was shown, in part, on a segment of *Unsolved Mysteries*. When Kelly visited the house where Johnston was raised, he recalled that he (Johnston) was only allowed to enter or leave the house via the back door. When they met Johnston's cousin, whose name was, indeed, Elizabeth, she confirmed that the boy was not allowed to use the front door. Then she asked if he remembered always eating the ends of bread loaves.

It is hard to imagine a more evidential regression case than this one. Kelly's memories of being Johnston are strong and clear. Brown noted Kelly's extreme and realistic discomfort when reliving Johnston's death. With the exception of the name of one crew member, no statement out of hundreds has been contradicted by research. The three full names of crewmen, the ship's name and number, and the date and location of the sinking were all recalled during the first regression session, before anyone had the chance to look up anything. The scores of facts and intimate details brought to light in later sessions and confirmed by independent investigation negate all feasibility of conspiracy or misrepresentation. Add the rapid alleviation of Kelly's symptoms and this is one of the most convincing cases yet examined.

One More Mission
[Case ID# 65, ESS Score = 286, Current Rank 1st]

Ian Stevenson, Dr. Jim Tucker, Carol Bowman and other researchers have uncovered hundreds of cases of children who inexplicably can recall living and dying as other people. The most impressive and thoroughly documented case yet, however, was brought to light not by the efforts of believers or even open-minded, objective scientists, but by a no-nonsense businessman, a stringent Christian, whose upbringing had hardened his mind against the idea of reincarnation.

Bruce Leininger reveled in research, a trait which served him well as a human-resource executive, handling personnel crises and developing corporate com-

pensation and insurance packages. When James, his
two-year-old son, started screaming and thrashing
about in the middle of the night, Bruce dismissed it as
no more than a nightmare, likely triggered by the un-
familiarity of his son's bedroom in their new home.
James had been moved before; just after his birth (on
April 10th 1998) the Leininger family had relocated
from the San Francisco area to Dallas, Texas, but he
was too young to remember that. Then, two months
previously, they had followed Bruce's job to Lafayette,
Louisiana. Some sort of reaction could be expected.
The screams were nothing to worry about, except that
Bruce needed his sleep.

Andrea Leininger, being expected to supply moth-
erly comfort and, therefore, an eyewitness to her toddler's nocturnal hysterics, could not so easily write
them off as a normal childhood nightmare. Up until
that night, James had been an unusually happy and
contented child who rarely cried or even fussed. The
next morning, she shared her concern with her husband, describing James' piercing shrieks and violent
kicking and flailing at the covers, but Bruce was indif-
ferent.

His lack of concern would, no doubt, have been
proper if James' performance hadn't been repeated
"with terrifying regularity and increasing frenzy."
They didn't happen every night – sometimes a night or
two would be skipped – but when one's sleep is disturbed four or five nights out of seven, the expectation

of a reoccurrence can ruin one's rest as well as the event itself. Andrea called her pediatrician, who told her the nightmares were normal night terrors and would soon diminish. She talked with friends; they agreed with her pediatrician. She conferred with her sisters, who echoed her friends and her pediatrician. Perhaps surprisingly, at least in retrospect, two months passed before Andrea realized that James was doing more than shrieking and thrashing about, he was also screaming words. When she caught the gist of what he was yelling, she ran down the hall and got her husband.

Bruce's annoyance at being dragged from bed evaporated quickly once he heard the words: "Airplane crash! Plane on fire! Little man can't get out!" These phrases were repeated over and over as little James flung his head back and forth and kicked upward wildly. Kicking, Andrea suddenly realized, just like a fighter pilot trying to kick his way out of a cockpit. Both mother and father were stunned; neither had any explanation.

Life went on as before.

The next bewildering incident occurred when Andrea gave James a toy airplane to distract him while she was shopping. "There's even a bomb on the bottom," she pointed out. "That's not a bomb, Mommy.

That's a dwop tank."[113] Andrea didn't know what a drop tank was. Bruce did. Neither had any idea how their toddler in diapers could identify one, even though he couldn't pronounce it properly.

On August 27th, after a long day playing with a friend from his pre-kindergarten class, James was being read a bedtime story when he casually said, "Mama, little man's airplane crash on fire." The Leiningers, having been told not to interrupt James' nightmares, had been waiting for an opportunity to question him while he was awake. Now, Andrea hurried to bring Bruce into the room.

Andrea asked, "Who is the little man?" James replied, "Me." Andrea asked, "Do you remember the little man's name?" James replied, "James." Thinking this was fruitless, Bruce tried a different tack, "Do you remember what kind of airplane the little man flew?" His son immediately replied, in the same conversational tone, "A Corsair." And from where did your plane take off? "A boat."

Now, perhaps James had seen a television program about Corsairs and aircraft carriers; although his mother claims he never watched anything but shows for little kids. And who's to say that James hadn't seen a drop tank when he and his dad visited an airplane museum back in Dallas? Of course, even if he had tak-

---

[113] A drop tank is an extra fuel tank that can be jettisoned when empty.

en notice of such an unobtrusive thing, he couldn't read signs, so he wouldn't have known what it was called. Nevertheless, all of this has been suggestive at best; not really proof of anything … so far.

Skeptics and debunkers should only proceed to read further at peril of their preconceptions.

Bruce asked his drowsy toddler the name of the boat he flew from. "Natoma," James replied. Bruce thought that sounded like a Japanese name and said so. Little James grew indignant and said no, it was American! Bruce, a bit taken aback that he had been challenged by someone who wasn't even potty trained, went to the Internet and discovered, to his amazement, that an American aircraft carrier called *Natoma Bay* had battled the Japanese in the Pacific.

Feeling that his religious beliefs and his role in the family were under fire, Bruce began a campaign to re-affirm both. He used the tool he knew best – tenacious research. Over the next few years, as little James re-vealed more and more about James the pilot, Bruce filled his dining room with letters, books, and boxes of documents about the war in the Pacific Theater. He traveled thousands of miles by car and plane and spent many hours on long-distance calls. Using the pretense of writing a book, he infiltrated the reunions of veter-ans of the *Natoma Bay* and its sister ships. He inter-viewed scores of old sailors and their family members. He was almost desperate to uncover some rational ex-planation for his son's memories — anything but the heresy of reincarnation. Andrea, although more accepting of reincarnation as an explanation, nevertheless spent considerable time helping to track down facts and people.

The following paragraphs summarize some of what was said by the child, James M. Leininger, and the confirmation his parents ultimately discovered.

Statement: The pilot's name was James, just like his. He often drew battle scenes with propeller-driven planes; he signed them "James 3" and explained, "Because I am the third James."

Fact: The only pilot on the *USS Natoma Bay* whose first name was James, was James M. Huston, Jr. [The second James?]

Statement: The American planes in his pictures were Wildcats and Corsairs.

Fact: Both were names of U.S. aircraft on carriers in WWII. The Wildcat was the plane Huston was piloting when he died. [Note: Several photographs relevant to this case are included in the write-up at www.SurvivalTop40.com.]

Statement: The red suns on some planes in his drawings meant they were Japanese.

Fact: The rising sun, depicted as a red circle, was the symbol of Imperial Japan.

Statement: The American sailors called Japanese fighters by boy names (such as Zekes) and bombers by girl names (such as Bettys).

Fact: Correct

Statement: He had a friend named Jack Larsen onboard the *USS Natoma Bay.*

Fact: Jack Larsen served on the *USS Natoma Bay* and was a friend of James Huston.

Statement: Unprompted, James pointed to a picture of Iwo Jima in a book and said that was where his plane was shot down.

Fact: James Huston's plane was the only one from the *Natoma Bay* that was shot down during the battle for Iwo Jima. [Huston was supposed to ship home the following day. He was not scheduled to make that run; he volunteered for one last mission when another pilot couldn't fly.]

Statement: Corsair planes had two defects: they often got flat tires and they wanted to turn left when they took off.

Fact: The Corsair's poor sight lines and heavy engines made for unusually rough landings on carrier decks, which blew an inordinate number of tires. The exceptional torque from their single front-mounted prop caused a drift to the left on takeoff. James Huston had served as a test pilot for Corsairs.

Statement: Three fellow crewmen, named Billy, Walter, and Leon, met him when he arrived in heaven. (He gave these names to his G.I. Joe action figures.)

Fact: In addition to James M. Huston, Jr., the names Billy Peeler, Walter Devlin, and Leon Conner were on the official list of men killed from the VC-81

Squadron aboard the *USS Natoma Bay*. Huston was killed on March 3, 1945. The other three died shortly prior to that, in late 1944.

Statement: His plane had been hit in the engine. (As soon as he could after receiving a new toy airplane he would crash it into the coffee table or some other hard surface and break off the propellers.)

Fact: An eyewitness to the crash of James Huston's plane said that the anti-aircraft fire blew away his propeller and his engine exploded as it went down.

Statement: While touring the Nimitz Museum, he saw a 5-inch cannon and announced that it was just like the gun on the fantail of the *Natoma Bay*.

Fact: The *USS Natoma Bay* had a 5-inch cannon on its fantail (the area of the hanger deck at the stern).

Statement: While watching a television program about Corsairs, James corrected the narrator by pointing out that the Japanese plane seen being shot down was a Tony, not a Zero. He explained that the Tony was a Japanese fighter that was smaller than a Zero.

Fact: True.

Statement: During his first telephone conversation with James Huston's sister, Anne Barron, who was 86 at the time, the 5-year-old James:

1. Called her Annie, even though his mom thought that disrespectful.

2. Said she had a sister "Roof" who was 4 years older than she.
3. Said her brother James was 4 years her junior.
4. Talked intimately and at length about the senior Huston's alcoholism and the devastating effects it had on the family.
5. Asked her what had happened to a picture of her that had been painted by their mother.

Fact: Only her long-dead brother, James Huston, Jr., ever called Anne Barron "Annie." She did have a sister (now deceased) named Ruth who was 4 years her senior. The painting, which no one else knew about, was in her attic. In short, everything little James said over the phone was correct and Anne Barron came to accept that the child was truly her brother born again.

As little James Leininger was encouraged to talk about his memories, the nightmares decreased in frequency, but continued sporadically for several years.

The evidence presented here should be more than enough to convince any open-minded person. The juxtaposition of "Natoma Bay" and "Jack Larsen" in the mind of a 2-year-old is, by itself, inexplicable by any other means than reincarnation or possession, either of which require Survival of the human memory and personality beyond the death of the body.

I will wrap this up by relating one more incident that may be the most intriguing of all. One day in

October of 2002, in response to a hug from his father, James commented, "When I found you and Mommy, I knew you would be good to me." (Note that this statement indicates that souls are independent, conscious beings prior to being born on earth, and so, on its own, is strongly suggestive of reincarnation.) "Where did you find us?" asked his father. "In Hawaii," James replied, "at the big pink hotel." Then he added that he had found them one night when they were eating dinner on the beach.

Five weeks before Andrea became pregnant with James, she and Bruce had celebrated their fifth wedding anniversary at the Royal Hawaiian, a landmark hotel easily recognized by its bright pink facade. On their last night there, they had eaten a dinner by moonlight on Waikiki Beach.

Sources
Memories of War

<u>Round Trip To Allentown</u>
The information in this case was adapted from a segment of
the television show *Sightings* broadcast on CBS on 6
May 1995.

<u>A Submariner Resurfaces</u>
Brown, Rick, "The Reincarnation of James, The Submarine
Man," *The Journal of Regression Therapy,* December, 1991,
pages 62-71.
"The Reincarnated Submariner," segment of *Unsolved
Mysteries* television series, this is included in the DVD
collection: *Unsolved Mysteries: Psychics.*

<u>One More Mission</u>
Leininger, Bruce and Andrea Leininger with Ken Gross, *Soul
Survivor: The Reincarnation of a World War II Fighter Pilot*,
Grand Central Publishing, 2009.
Various videos of interviews with the Leiningers, available
on YouTube.

Moving On

In interviews and discussions, I am often asked, "Do you really believe this stuff?" To which, my answer is, "No. I don't believe any of it."

My statement is met with varied looks and exclamations — sometimes of consternation (as if I was crazy), sometimes of triumph (as if the interviewer had finally gotten me to admit to fraud).

But, in the next moment, I always add, "Believing is thinking a certain thing when there are insufficient facts to back up your thoughts. So, no, I do not *believe* in the continuation of the human personality after the demise of the physical body. Rather, I have carefully examined the evidence and rationally reached the logical conclusion that the afterlife is real — beyond a reasonable doubt!

That phrase — "beyond a reasonable doubt" — is important, for it suggests a legal venue for any arguments about the validity or acceptability of the evidence. In such a courtroom setting, there is no place for statements as to whether or not there is "scientific" proof of an afterlife. Science is a most useful system for evaluating purely physical events; but it does not deal in "proofs" (other than in mathematics) and is useless when non-physical factors (such as spirits) may arbitrarily and surreptitiously affect its experiments.

Instead, the search for the truth in matters of the spiritual and the psychic must and should depend on well-established legalistic tests of the strength of evidence and the reliability of witnesses. These procedures have been employed for centuries to determine guilt or innocence; to set men free or send them to the gallows. When we apply them to the vast array of solid evidence for Survival, the verdict is clear: Death is but a doorway to other realms of existence.

At Gettysburg, on the 3rd of July 1863, General Robert E. Lee commanded his troops to charge across Seminary Ridge into the teeth of the Union lines. In the next 60 minutes, some 5,000 Confederate soldiers died in what became known as Pickett's charge. This was the beginning of the end of one of the bloodiest wars in history. I wonder if Lee, or any commanding officer, would ever send another man into battle if they fully comprehended the process of self-judgement and empathic agony that awaits us all on the other side of death. For that matter, how could anyone ever agitate for war if they have any inkling of what awaits them in the next realm? How could they ever condone slavery or ignore poverty if they understood that we spirits come back to live on earth again and again in every race and every role? Can you imagine a world in which everyone realizes that they are part of one, vast spiritual family?

Each of us could pursue no activity more worthy than affirming this great truth.

For more on this topic, its implications, and opportunities, please visit the website of the Association for Evaluation and Communication of Evidence for Survival (AECES) at www.aeces.info.

The 'Sin' of Speaking with Spirits

S ome people have concerns about sitting with a medium or consulting a psychic because they think that doing so puts them at odds with certain teachings in the Bible.

The main support for this belief in the Old Testament is from the book known as Leviticus. The key verse (generally labeled 19:31) says, "Do not turn to mediums or wizards, do not seek them out to be defiled by them."

There is another verse in Leviticus and one in Deuteronomy that clearly judge those who make a practice of talking to dead people: "A man or woman who is a medium or a wizard shall be put to death;" and "There shall not be found among you any one who ... is a medium [for they are] an abomination to the Lord."[114]

There can be no doubt that these statements are in the Bible and that they distinctly prohibit consultations with the spirit world. If you accept Leviticus and Deuteronomy as the inerrant word of the Almighty, then you would be wise to avoid any contact with mediums or psychics. But, before you make such a decision, you

---

[114] Lev 20:27 and Deut 18:10.

might want to know what else you are signing on for. There are numerous other things that are likewise prohibited by these ancient writings.

Have you ever eaten a rare steak? Or a fatty hamburger? Have you ever trimmed your hair or beard? Did you ever get a tattoo; peek at your brother in the nude; fail to stand when an old man enters the room? Have you ever worn a shirt of cotton and polyester blend? Perhaps you have been upset with the government and cursed a politician? According to the Old Testament,[115] all of these acts and many others are sins against the Lord and are condemned just as strongly as consulting a medium.

And if you actually *are* a medium, do you deserve to die? These books say you do. But they also condemn you to immediate execution if you ever had an affair with a neighbor, or used withdrawal as a form of birth control, or had a homosexual encounter.[116] Think you're safe because you never went in for such hanky-panky? Well did you ever happen to get angry with mom or dad and curse them or disobey them?[117] According to the Old Testament, if you've done any of these things, you are already just as doomed as you would be if you helped someone converse with their dear departed grandmother.

---

[115] Lev 19:26, 3:17, 19:27, 19:28, 20:17, 19:32; 19:19; Ex 22:28.

[116] Lev 20:10; Gen 38:9; Lev 20:13.

[117] Levi 20:9; Deut 21:18.

Still think you should follow the dictates of the ancient Hebrew tribesmen? Well then, perhaps you would be interested in learning the proper procedure for selling your daughter into slavery; that's covered in Exodus 21:7-11.

Why and how the Old Testament came to have such pernicious laws is too long a story to tell here. Suffice it to say that it is a tale of nepotism and greed beyond what any big-city politician would dare emulate today. No matter the rationale, though, there is no authority in selectively citing passages that support your point of view while blatantly violating or completely ignoring scores of other definite rules clearly laid down by the same priesthood.

For the sake of this article, I am going to assume that the reader would agree with me that being stoned to death is not an appropriate penalty for disobeying one's parents. (Although as a parent I have sometimes wavered in that view, I admit that I wouldn't be here to write this if such a law had been in force during my own teenage rebellions.) Most reasonable people will likewise find the bulk of these Old Testament strictures to be overly harsh, if not abhorrent. If you can be comfortable getting your hair cut, then you should have no qualms about visiting a medium.

Another, less direct, argument against mediumship is that dead people cannot talk, therefore all communications are actually with demons who are trying to deceive the living and lead them away from

God's word. The verses most often cited are these from Psalms: "For in death there is no remembrance of thee; in Sheol who can give thee praise?" and "The dead do not praise the Lord nor do any that go down into silence."[118]

In truth, these are the words of a poet addressing his Creator and imploring Him to "Help me now; Don't wait 'til I'm dead." The author clearly is not God (Would He be composing pleas to Himself?) and is not claiming any special knowledge beyond the rather primitive beliefs of his fellow tribesmen. Besides, these exhortations could just as easily be read to imply that spirits *do* still exist and *are* capable of receiving favors.

Also note that the writers of the Old Testament did not connect the idea of mediums or spirits with either demons or the devil; that idea came along much later. The serpent in the Garden of Eden represented wisdom and is not linked to the devil or even to evil. The Satan so prominent in the book of Job is more of a prosecuting attorney charged with testing God's creations, he is given no power to wreck havoc on his own. Satan is mentioned, without description or comment, only two other times (Chronicles 21:1 and Zechariah 3:1-2). The term "demons" likewise only appears twice (Deut 32:17 and Psalms 106:37) and each time seems to be simply another term for false gods that the fickle Hebrews were punished for worshiping.

---

[118] Psalms 6:5 and 115:17.

And then there is the matter of "by their fruits you shall know them." If the results of a spirit communication are alleviation of grief, enhanced compassion, reduction of anxiety, a feeling of being closer to God, and other such positive feelings and actions, then what role could the devil be playing? What sort of demon goes around encouraging folks to love one another?

Now, this is not to say that all dead people are good people. Experience teaches the opposite; people don't tend to change very much when they die. Nasty folks can thus become nasty spirits. So, it's wise to be cautious, especially when attempting contact on one's own. In more succinct terms: "Test the spirits."

Which leads us to the New Testament.

Nothing in the New Testament admonishes us not to visit mediums or speak with the spirits of departed friends and relatives.

The earliest writings in this collection are seven letters written by Paul. (Another seven letters are commonly titled as being Paul's writing, but were likely written by others.[119]) The earliest of these, and thus the earliest known document referencing Jesus, is *First Thessalonians*. In this letter, Paul encourages his readers, "Do not despise prophetic utterances, but bring them all to the test and keep what is good in them and

---

[119] These are not exactly examples of plagiarism, but rather have been labeled as letters written "in the tradition of Paul" by early scribes. See *From Jesus to Christ* by Paula Fredriksen, Ph.D., 1988.

avoid the bad."[120] Paul's next surviving missive is *First Corinthians*, wherein he claims: "In each of us the Spirit is manifested in one particular way, for some useful purpose. One man, through the Spirit has ... gifts of healing, and another miraculous powers; another has the gift of prophecy, and another the ability to distinguish true spirits from false."[121] And in *1 John*, we are advised, "Do not trust any and every spirit, test the spirits to see whether they are from God."[122]

Such admonishments seem to indicate that early Christians spent much of their time in their meetings making ecstatic utterances and prophesying. The only concern that the apostles had is that their followers may be listening to the wrong spirits. This is a most significant shift from the attitudes expressed in the Old Testament. Previously, anyone who approached the tabernacle without specific authorization would be struck dead by Jehovah Himself. Although a prophet's voice would occasionally be recognized as legitimate – so long as he concentrated on warning the Israelites to obey Jehovah or face terrible retribution – that's a far cry from encouraging everyman to converse directly with the Almighty. This change of attitude is likely because the early Christians had no entrenched priest-

---

[120] I Thessalonians 5:19-20.

[121] I Corinthians 12:8-10.

[122] 1 John 4:1.

hood that jealously guarded their exclusive (and highly profitable) rights to divine contact.

Recommended Readın

The sources consulted in writing this book are citeq
the appropriate pages. Rather than repeat them here, I
thought it might be more useful to my readers to provide a list of the books that I would want my students
to read if I were to be teaching a course in Survival.
Other than this book and its prequel (*The Survival Files*)
here are the best of the best. List is in alphabetical order by title.

*Afterlife Encounters: Ordinary People, Extraordinary Expe-
riences*, by Dianne Arcangel. Of the many books
detailing after-death communications this is the
best because the cases are well-written, carefully
documented, and thoughtfully presented.

The Afterlife Experiments, by Gary Schwartz, Ph.D.
Scientists test John Edward, George Anderson, and
other contemporary mediums under controlled
laboratory conditions.

The Articulate Dead, by Michael E. Tymn. A masterful
job of selecting the people and events of most importance to the history of survival research and
presenting them is an easily comprehended and
most entertaining manner.

onscious Universe: The Scientific Truth of Psychic Phenomena, by Dean Radin, Ph.D. A scientist takes a careful look at the scientific evidence. Many of the revelations and conclusions are surprising.

Exploring Reincarnation, by Hans TenDam. The definitive work on reincarnation; scholarly yet quite readable, with numerous intriguing case histories.

Journey Of Souls: Case Studies of Life Between Lives, by Michael Newton, Ph.D. Doctor Newton has developed a technique of regression that is long, difficult, and uniquely productive. With it, he gets subjects to recall what few can otherwise recall — the time they spend between lives.

Lessons From The Light by Kenneth Ring, Ph.D. The all-around best book on Near-Death Experiences (NDEs); their characteristics, their meaning, and their impacts. Includes a compelling chapter on NDEs by children.

There Is No Death and There Are No Dead, by Tom and Lisa Butler. The directors of the largest organization studying electronic voice phenomena (a.k.a. instrumental trans-communication) have created an encyclopedic work detailing all aspects of using electronic devices to commune with departed souls. Covers history, examples, and technique.

Appendix Three

The Evidence Scoring System

The ESS is a system for objectively determining what cases provide the most convincing evidence for Survival of the human personality after the demise of the physical body.

Purpose

There are thousands of cases on record that have been cited by one expert or another as being good evidence for the existence of an afterlife, that is for "Survival" (with a capital S). Up until now, there has been significant disagreement as to which cases make the very best evidence. Although we recognize that the inherent differences among people will always ensure a wide range of personal preferences, we think that a consistent, coherent, and objective system for ranking these cases will enable a clearer and more concerted educational effort. The more agreement that researchers and communicators can demonstrate, the more efficient their work and the more effective their message.

Coverage Exclusions

To minimize damage to the list in the most unlikely – but possible – event that credible doubt is cast on the veracity of a source, no more than three cases from the same source may be part of the Top 40 at any given time.

Any case that has an indication of improper influence, tampering, or fraud is rejected and not considered under this system.

OBEs (Out-of-Body, or Other-Body, Experiences) are limited to people who continue to live. While certainly suggestive of a spirit world, of themselves they are not good evidence of what happens after the body dies and, thus, are not considered herein unless they involve the reception of confirmable information known only to discarnate beings.

This system does not cover arguments for Survival based on deductions from observations of human behavior. For instance the origin of musical genius in children or the origin of unexplained experiential referents in the blind or deaf. Furthermore there are certain characteristics that automatically remove a case from consideration, no matter how strong it may be otherwise. These disqualifying characteristics are:

- **Hard To Comprehend**. If readers have to puzzle out a case, they will assume that they are missing something, and assume that that "something" is the explanation, rather than contact with spirits. This is why the cross-correspondences will never make good evidence for any but the most erudite.
- **Hints of Deception**. Any association with magic or illusion will seriously undermine confidence in the evidence, no matter how deserving of confidence that evidence might be. This is one reason why physical mediumship will never convince an unbeliever. Not even when filmed with six cameras

in broad daylight. After all, if David Copperfield can do it . . . ?

Nothing is more closely associated with deception than darkness. One is justified in being reticent to accept any effect that requires turning out the lights. There are dozens of cases of poltergeist and similar activity in which solid objects levitate, fly around in controlled patterns, appear, and disappear in lighted rooms and outdoors in the daytime. Furthermore, there are mediums, such as Sophia Williams and Elizabeth Blake, whose direct voices have managed quite well in normal room light.

Those physical mediums who will not even allow filming with infrared or other passive systems are asking to be approached with the utmost incredulity.

Nevertheless, the above does not rule out consideration of cases in which inexplicable information is provided by a medium who happens to be in a darkened room.

• **Outrageous Personages**. Skeptics often denigrate reincarnation by asserting (falsely) that most people recall lives of famous people. Although it is certainly possible that Napoleon or Lincoln may be born again, any case in which someone claimed such a provenance are automatically rejected. Likewise, cases wherein famous people speak through mediums — although they may be true— are so outlandish that they have no power to convince. Moreover, these cases are worse than use-less, because they provide the skeptics with such easy targets for derision.

- **Offensive or Disgusting**. Few people can retain open, objective attitudes in the face of goopy stuff oozing from ears or rods extending from abdo-mens. If one's audience is grossed out, they'll ne-ver be convinced.

- **Political or Social Agendas**. Cases that seem to pro-mote causes or try to change the behavior of the listener will always be viewed with suspicion. Bla-tant attempts to gain followers are, of course, the most distrusted; but moral, ethical, and even envi-ronmental discourses can also raise suspicions and detract from the evidential value of an incident.

- **Alien Suspects**. If there is any evidence or testimony suggesting that the incident was the result of the use of super-advanced technology – whether ex-tra-terrestrial, extra-dimensional, or otherwise al-ien – then the case is outside the scope of the ESS and will not be ranked; nor will it be considered for the Survival Top Forty.

Scoring

Cases that seem legitimate are assigned a number, according to the value earned under two parameters.

The first parameter (CS) is the certainty of the source being discarnate. That is, how likely are possi-ble alternatives that might explain the information be-ing communicated or the occurrence of the incident. The less likely the alternatives, the higher the CS rat-ing. This is the main scale and can be used alone.

The second parameter (WR) indicates the reliability of the report on which the case is based. Having a separate score allows evaluators to see if there are any correlations between who is telling the stories and how evidential are the tales. It also provides a means to distinguish rank between cases with equal CS scores.

For WR, the highest possible value is 100. The CS parameter, being most critical, is weighted heavier (up to a maximum of 200).

Ranking Principles

The evidential value for most cases depends on the existence and probability of alternative sources for the information imparted or alternative causes for the incidents. No case is considered if a prosaic explanation is apparent or reasonably suspected. Therefore, the possible alternatives involve degrees of paranormal powers varying from receiving the projected thoughts of an involved individual to tapping directly into an omniscient cosmic consciousness to causing solid objects to dematerialize.

To better understand this concept, imagine that a young man goes to see a medium whom he has never met before. The medium goes into a trance and gives the man various bits of information. If we were to rank those facts according to the difficulty of psychically acquiring the information (without input from the spirit world), our list might look like this:

- The name of a departed friend from whom the sitter hoped to hear. (Reading an involved person's thoughts.)
- The name of the departed friend's fiancé, whom the sitter was not thinking about. (Reading an involved person's conscious mind.)
- The name of the departed friend's first dog, which the sitter had once known but cannot now recall. (Reading an involved person's unconscious mind.)
- That the departed friend had a brother who died in infancy; a fact the sitter had never known. (Reading the mind of an uninvolved person, *e.g.* a still living relative of the sitter's friend.)
- Where the departed friend had hidden some money; a fact that no one else but the friend knew. (Pulling information from a cosmic data bank.)
- That the departed friend's grave marker had been damaged by lightning the day before; a fact that was never known to any person while living. (No alternative explanation conceivable.)

It should be pointed out here that the act of mental telepathy is, in and of itself, strong evidence for the existence of a non-physical plane of consciousness, and thus is indirect evidence of Survival. The problem with telepathy is not in the transmission or the reception but in the tuning. It isn't so difficult to accept that we can mentally send and receive thoughts; it is virtually impossible to imagine how a mind, acting alone, could sort through all the billions of thoughts that are being sent out at any given moment and read only the sought-for message. Without some structure, all that any mind could ever receive is the 'white noise' created by the intermingling of the thoughts of every being in the universe. This argues strongly for the existence of some sort of universal mind or discarnate communications system that routes and delivers mental images according to our intention or desire. Such a system couldn't be limited to our own minds; it would have to exist in a mental plane independent of the physical.

The same is true for other non-local mental powers such as remote-viewing. Some have conjectured that remote-viewing could account for obtaining information that does not reside in a living mind, but this is most unlikely. Successful remote-viewing procedures require that a target be consciously selected and then carefully concentrated on. If a skilled practitioner were given the coordinates of a particular grave, he might be able to 'view' it and report back as to whether the headstone appeared to have been struck by lightning. But even then, the ability to wend one's mental way through the vastness of the universe to a specific spot demands the existence of some sort of map and navigation system. So, we're right back to the requirement for a cosmic consciousness.

Without being given a specific target, there is no conceivable way that a medium's mind, operating solo, could first sense that something had been struck by lightning, then identify what it was and who it belonged to, and then discover its placement. Such a feat could only be achieved with the guidance of someone who already knew the location and had observed the damage (presumably, the spirit of the person whose body was buried in that grave).

Information is not limited to facts about the four w's (who, what, where, and when). It also can be in the form of how. For instance, if a person who has never played chess instantaneously acquires master-level skill at the game, they have received a great deal of information that might only be explained by spirit involvement.

In addition to cases involving the communication of information, there are some very convincing cases that simply involve some unusual or inexplicable occurrence that, of itself, indicates the presence of a departed spirit. In a manner similar to the "information cases," these are rated according to how difficult it might be to reproduce the effect by mental powers alone. Thus, a radio turning on "by itself" is considered less evidential than a tape cassette disappearing in front of one's eyes, because it is intuitively easier to affect electrical systems by "mind power" than it is to alter the basic structure/existence of materials. Nevertheless, the analyst must remember that we have no solid evidence that spirits residing in physical bodies somehow gain marvelous powers upon leaving those bodies. We must always ask, therefore, why the effect could not have been caused by the unconscious mind of a living person.

Then there are the instances when the image of a departed person (a ghost or apparition) is observed. If the observer was familiar with the appearance of the deceased, then a memory-based hallucination might be the cause, and the case will not be convincing. If the observer had never seen the person (or a picture of the person) yet is able to describe the person in sufficient detail for others to recognize the person, then we have a strong case for Survival. The case becomes even stronger if the apparition appears at a time and place of significance, such as the deathbed of a spouse. Such a well-timed visitation indicates both awareness and volition on the spirit's part.

Meaning of Low Scores

A low score for a particular case does not mean that it is false or dubious in any way. (As indicated above, if there is reason to suspect deception, then the case would not be considered for scoring.) Nor is a low-scoring case deemed without value or merit to believers. A low score simply indicates that the case does not make a very effective argument when trying to convince an uninformed or dubious public of the existence of life after death.

Determining the Scores

The Certainty of Discarnate Source (CS) and Witness Reliability (WR) scores are derived by following a path through a collection of questions, most of which can be answered either "yes" or "no," the answer determining the next question to be answered and the number of points (if any) to be deducted from the base score. A few questions prompt the user to choose from a short list of options. Altogether, these "decision trees" provide an objective and replicable means of assigning a numeric score to both parameters.

The actual decision trees used in the ESS consist of 20 pages (office size) of tables. These are not suitable for display or reading in a book of this size. Thus, the full ESS document is available for download from www.SurvivalTop40.com, also accessible via www .aeces.info.

Index of Personal Names

Names known to be pseudonyms are marked with [p].